PENGUIN BOOKS

YOU WILL BE ALRIGHT

Sonali Gupta is one of India's leading psychotherapists with two decades of experience. Working at the intersection of relationships, grief and compassion, she consults with young adults, artistes, couples, NGOs and corporates to enhance their emotional well-being. She is a consultant with Spotify India on Project Pause, which focuses on mental health. Her columns around building a culture of mental health have been part of both national and local newspapers consistently for the last decade.

Sonali was awarded the Elle Mental Wellness Expert Award for 2023 and won the Cosmopolitan Mental Health Advocate Award for the year 2023–24.

Her work and expertise have been recognized by mainstream media, and she is deeply loved and respected within the mental health community.

With over 1,00,000 subscribers, her YouTube channel, Mental Health with Sonali, is one of the largest for a mental health professional in India. Sonali's first book *Anxiety: Overcome It and Live without Fear* was published in 2020. This is her second book.

ADVANCE PRAISE FOR THE BOOK

'A compassionate, insightful book for anyone looking to heal from the complexities of loss, *You Will Be Alright* by Sonali Gupta is a beacon of hope and wisdom'—**Dr Shyam Bhat, MD and founder, Nirvikalpa: The Mind-Body Centre**

'*You Will Be Alright: A Guide to Navigating Grief* by Sonali Gupta is a compassionate and practical guide to understanding and coping with loss, especially in the Indian context. Drawing on her extensive experience, Sonali offers simple, clear explanations and valuable tools to help readers through their grief journey. This book is a beacon of hope and support for anyone dealing with loss'—**Sonali Bendre, actor and author**

'This book is empathetic, insightful and will guide the reader to understand grief as a process rather than a condition. Sonali has created a safe space for healing where everyone can find something of great value'—**Dia Mirza, actor, producer, United Nations SDGs advocate and eco-investor**

'Sonali has a deep understanding and years of experience through her work in dealing with grief and helping her clients. I am glad there is now a book available as a go-to resource for anyone. The book is written with sensitivity and it offers hope, and a vocabulary to talk about grief in a culture where silence is the norm. This wonderful volume will help you deal with grief and develop a deeper understanding of your own self'—**Guneet Monga Kapoor, Academy Award winner and film producer**

YOU WILL BE ALRIGHT

A GUIDE TO NAVIGATING GRIEF

SONALI GUPTA

PENGUIN BOOKS
An imprint of Penguin Random House

PENGUIN BOOKS

Penguin Books is an imprint of the Penguin Random House group of companies
whose addresses can be found at global.penguinrandomhouse.com

Published by Penguin Random House India Pvt. Ltd
4th Floor, Capital Tower 1, MG Road,
Gurugram 122 002, Haryana, India

Penguin Random House India

First published in Penguin Books by Penguin Random House India 2024

10 9 8 7 6 5 4 3 2 1

ISBN 9780143460206

www.penguin.co.in

To my father, who in his illness and death taught me how to live.
To my mother, who holds us together with her
quiet presence and unconditional love.

'It's an honour to be in grief. It's an honour to feel that much, to have loved that much.'

—Elizabeth Gilbert

Contents

Part 5: Together We Will Be Alright

Disclaimer

The perspectives and understanding of loss shared in the book are based on the author's own research and personal experience of grief, as well as the learnings and exploration of work done by psychologists around loss over the years. The author has also included reflections that have emerged from working with her clients in therapy over the last two decades. However, readers are cautioned that these views may not work for everyone. The content and information provided in this book is intended to help readers in their individual journeys as they try to make sense of grief and grieving. However, the same is in no way a substitute for individual therapy. The publisher or author assume no responsibility or liability for any errors, inaccuracies or omissions contained in the book. The publisher and the author make no representations or warranties of any kind with respect to this book or its contents. All liability from the adoption of perspectives and tools discussed in this book is expressly disclaimed by the publisher and the author. This book is for informational purposes only and is not intended as a substitute for consultation with a licensed medical/mental health practitioner. The names, ages and other identifying details relating to the author's clients have been changed to protect their privacy.

How to Read This Book

Grief can be overwhelming and sneaky.

The idea here is, therefore, not to instruct you on how you should be reading the book. Instead, the idea is to create a space in which you can feel the freedom and autonomy to choose what parts of your grief you want to attend to at this moment, and what are the parts that you want to maybe come back to at a later stage.

I'm aware that getting around to reading the book can be overwhelming for some of you. So, as you read the book, pause and take a break and maybe re-read some parts that either resonate with or cause dissonance for you.

Grief is very personal, so the idea is not for you to absorb and integrate everything that's stated. Instead, choose to stay with the information and let it marinate. You can choose to ignore the parts that don't make sense to you.

Each section is independent in a way, although it may have some references that are about topics covered either in the previous or forthcoming sections.

If you want to try and understand the vocabulary of grief, begin with the first section. It is a glimpse into unpacking the terms that generally surround us when we find ourselves faced with loss. If you are cerebral and want to do a deep dive into understanding the science of grief, then the theories in the first section might work for you. The second section is an exploration of grief that we don't understand and speaks about vicarious and collective grief.

The third and fourth sections are all about questions that stare at us as we try to understand what grief means to us and move forward. These sections are about what continues to linger for us, whether it's internally or in the external world—reminding us again and again that our world has changed in the aftermath of loss. If that's where you are, begin with these sections.

If you are supporting someone who is dealing with grief, then begin with the fifth section, which is about how we can be there for others, what to say and what not to say.

I hope that the book serves as an anchor for all of you dealing with grief. Remember, the book is going to be here, so choose your pace.

You know best how much and what you want to read.

Introduction

No One Ever Told Me about Grief

I was about eight or nine years old when my father was first hospitalized. He had diabetes, which was not managed. As a result, he had developed complications. As I grew up, the period between the hospitalizations kept becoming shorter and shorter and the illness began impacting his other organs. As a child, I felt worried and scared, and my anxiety felt like a low-grade fever that was always present. I wondered what would happen. How long would he survive? Would he die?

We lived in a joint family with my grandparents, parents and my younger brother. No one in the family ever spoke openly about my father's illness to my brother and me. This seemed extremely strange, because both my brother and I were very close to our mum and grandparents. My father had several surgeries and came close to a foot amputation when I was fifteen. However, his foot was saved by a wise doctor. Later, dialysis and a fall left him bedridden. Finally, in 2013, a week after he had turned sixty and when I was thirty-three, he passed away due to organ failure. He himself knew he was not going to live very long; he could feel it, but none of us believed it.

When my father passed away on 9 May 2013, I realized that all those years of undergoing what felt like anxiety was grief all along. Although I had been in therapy and under supervision for years, no one had spelt it out for me. Just the naming of the feeling centred me and made me realize that grief as an emotion goes beyond death. I also realized what we don't name and acknowledge controls us. Over the years, it had become a part of me. Always there.

Now, years later, when I work at the intersection of grief, relationships and resilience, I have begun to realize that families across the globe don't really talk about death and the feeling of grief that surrounds us. So many of my clients in therapy over the years have spoken about how they experienced early losses of either their sibling, parent or even a pet—and yet there had been a silence around it. Here are some instances of what clients have shared with me in therapy sessions.

Mayuri, a forty-three-year-old, told me, 'This is the first time in years that I am crying while thinking about my mother's death. I was six when my mother died in an accident. No one asked me how I felt or even tried to talk to me about what I was feeling. At home, there was sadness; yet my dad made it feel like life must go on. I was not allowed to go to the funeral.'

Ronak, a forty-eight-year-old man, who started therapy primarily because he felt that sadness has been lurking within him for years since he was a child, shared with me, 'Dad was sick for a couple of years and dealing with cancer. He was in and out of hospitals. Then, one fine day, when I came home from my friend's house after playing, I was told he's no more. That's it. I was twelve. I feel angry that if he was dying, why had no one told me before? I knew he was unwell, but I wish someone had told me that we needed to say our goodbyes. I would have hugged him longer, told him how much I loved him and how I would miss our guitar lessons together.'

These two client experiences and the personal story that I share are reminders that in some form or another, maybe many of us have been in life situations where our loved ones, despite their best intentions, just didn't talk to us about grief. My hypothesis is that maybe no one ever talked to them, either and that's why they didn't know any better. What I came to observe and experience is that there is a culture of intergenerational silence that surrounds grief.

As a society, we fail to acknowledge grief. Sometimes, I wonder if the word 'grief' takes the form of 'something that shouldn't be named'. It is as if people believe that acknowledging their loss and naming it would bring bad luck or make them not-so-good people. As a child, I wondered if thinking about my dad's demise meant that I was asking or wishing for an unfortunate event to happen. I remember carrying so much guilt within as I wondered how long my father would live.

One of the big reasons for writing this book is to address the silence that surrounds grief, to talk about myths around loss and grieving and to build a vocabulary around what we are feeling when we grieve. My clients consistently tell me that there is a lack of vocabulary when it comes to understanding grief. I was spurred to write this book when my clients nudged me to pen something from an Indian perspective, reminding me that I needed to put down some of my understanding and insights for all those who may or may not have access to therapy.

The book has a lot of references to my clients' struggles and their inner journeys as they dealt with grief and worked towards its integration. The word 'client' doesn't do any justice to the therapy relationship. However, I find the term 'patient' very labelling, so I have made a choice to refer to them as 'clients' throughout the book. The references used in the book are from my clinical practice and experience from 2004 to 2024.

Part 1

Understanding Grief and How It Affects Us

1

Unpacking Myths

'No one seems to understand grief, yet everyone seems to have advice for me.'

'After my brother's death, there has been tremendous grief, but I don't know how to express it, what to say and I'm not even sure if what I'm experiencing is normal.'

These statements are reflective of what I hear from my clients repeatedly, when they experience grief. The biggest challenge that people seem to bring to therapy is how there isn't a clear vocabulary or understanding that others have about the nature of grief. This lack of understanding in turn leads to people carrying forward myths and personal ideas, which often come in the way of dealing with grief.

Over my two decades of work as a therapist, I have been asked some questions over and over by clients. They hope the answers will help them fathom and process their grief better. This chapter is an exploration of those questions and my own understanding around it. There is space after each segment for you to write down your own insights, memories and personal truths.

Myth: There are some people who have never experienced grief.

Fact: Grief is something each one of us has experienced. The very fact that we are human means that we will experience loss. We may not have acknowledged it, had the vocabulary for it or allowed ourselves to feel it, but we all have encountered it.

Myth: We only experience grief when we lose a loved one to death.

Fact: While we often look at grief in the context of losing a loved one to death, grief at its very core is associated with a feeling of loss. We all have experienced loss at some stage of our life, in some form or another. So, whether it's a break-up, separation, loss of autonomy, illness, infertility, recognizing that a partner is having an affair—in all these moments, we experience grief. The reality is that for very long, people don't even recognize that they are experiencing grief.

We may grieve not just when we lose a loved one but also for absolute strangers who die tragically, for children who died in accidents or due to illness, those who died by suicide and when our favourite authors or celebrities pass away. During the pandemic, we experienced collective grief. It was a moment in time when we all felt strangely connected by this thread.

Myth: Everyone who experiences grief has a language and vocabulary for it.

Fact: Most of us don't have a language or even a vocabulary for grief. As we begin to make sense of our grief and process it, we begin to get better at developing a vocabulary and an understanding of what it means and entails. It is okay if you don't understand it and take time to fathom it. It is part of the grieving process, so learn to be kind to your own self.

Myth: We can recover from grief and get done with it as time passes.

Fact: Unlike other emotions, which come and go, grief stays with us. It's not a phase that we get done with or move on from. David Kessler, an author and expert on grief, says that grief is not flu, which we can recover from. Yet, we as human beings have the capacity to integrate and process grief and learn to rebuild our life. Grief stays, yet with time, it feels different. We learn to live with it.

Myth: Because we have experienced grief, we can fully understand what grief means for others.

Fact: While we all experience grief, how it is felt in our bodies and minds is very subjective. Our experience of grief may allow us to have a sense of what it is for others to go through it, but it is so complex that no two individuals grieve the same way. What is important is that while each one of us have our own share of grief, how we experience it is very personal. So, while we may have understood and felt grief, we still never really can fully comprehend what grief evokes for others, and how they would experience it in their bodies, minds and souls. Recognizing this is the first step in being present for anyone and their reality at a time of grief. There are so many factors and conditions, along with our own personality, that impact how we grieve and in turn how we process it.

Myth: Once people begin to feel hope, grief is dealt with.

Fact: How people cope with grief is deeply personal. While it sounds extremely difficult and hard to comprehend, **the reality is that grief and hope can be held together.** We can feel extremely helpless and hopeless on one day as we grieve, and yet as we begin to process, we can hold space for grief and also for hope. If you have felt this, I would encourage you to think about it here. If you have never experienced that, I want you to know that it's possible and let this thought anchor you in your own journey towards that hope.

Myth: You should be able to deal with the loss in nine months to a year.

Fact: There is no timeline when it comes to grief. While people may do the work of moving forward in their life, readapting their life and making a new beginning, that doesn't mean that people have dealt with the grief. It is a very personal process, and we may never reach a place when grief is fully dealt with. But that's alright. We learn to build our life around our grief. Our love stays and, in that sense, grief is love that continues to linger.

Activity

When you were dealing with grief, were there any myths that you encountered? Take a few minutes to think and pen it down for yourself.

____

____

____

2

What Is Grief?

Psychiatrist Dr Colin Murray Parkes in his book, *Bereavement: Studies of Grief in Adult Life*, says, 'The pain of grief is just as much a part of life as the joy of love; it is, perhaps, the price we pay for love, the cost of commitment.'[1]

When we lose anything that we have beautifully worked towards or loved, either to death or other reasons, we experience grief. At its very core, grief comes with the feeling of absence that we either experience or fear that we may.

Grief is what we feel when we experience loss. At the heart of grief is a feeling of love that continues to exist, and yet the person who we feel love for is 'no more'. Clients, while describing their grief to me, have made statements like the ones listed below:

'My world came crashing down.'

'The ground on which I was standing suddenly felt shaky and it was as if the rug was pulled away.'

'It felt as if I had lost a limb.'

'The pain I felt was unbearable and it all seemed purposeless; I was helpless.'

'It felt like my world was falling apart and I didn't know who I was without my partner.'

'I couldn't believe it, it all kept feeling like a bad dream.'

With grief, people very often use the word 'heartbroken', a reminder of how something within us breaks. We are no longer the same. Just as our loved one's presence shapes us and determines who we are, their absence impacts us similarly, in ways we may not be able to comprehend.

Our grief is felt as a breakdown of all that we knew and constructed our world around. When our loved one dies, it feels like a part of us and who we are also dies with them. It feels like the world, the way we knew it and experienced it, is no longer the same. If you are feeling this, then I understand you. Grief often comes with multiple feelings all at once, and hence it is all-consuming. Shock, sadness, fear, anger, helplessness, a sharp longing for the person who has passed away, yearning for them and somewhere knowing that nothing can be done—it is all of these emotions.

Is Grief Limited to Losing a Loved One to Death?

For years, grief has remained synonymous with losing loved ones to death. At the same time, think about women in fertility clinics, faces at the family court and other such instances—a consistent reminder of what could have been, dealing with their losses as they try to move on.

Over the years as I worked in therapy, I began to realize that at any given time, a large number of my clients were dealing with grief. All of them had lost a loved one, but not necessarily to death. There was loss either due to divorce, separation, a break-up, a slow fading away of close friendship, grief experienced in relation to climate change and much more. What was still common to all these clients was a sense of loss, a yearning for what they had lost and a deep sadness. To each of them, it felt all-consuming; most clients would describe it as a visceral feeling. They could feel it in their bones and yet, it was hard to explain to others what exactly they were feeling.

Around 2015, I made a conscious choice to focus on work around relationships and intimacy. A year after I began working consistently around relationship dynamics, I realized that a large portion of the work I was doing was around grief. Somehow, when I made the choice, I never thought that work on relationships would entail so much handling of grief. **I have begun to realize that all relationship work is grief work.**

At that point, I recognized that grief is our response when we lose a loved one to death and at the same time, it's also what we experience when we drift away from an old friend, have a miscarriage, experience a relationship ending, when we lose something that was familiar or when there is betrayal. Where there is love, there is a possibility of grief in some way or another. Maybe therefore sometimes, we are so scared to love.

Grief is what we feel when we experience loss. Losses take various forms. This idea has existed in psychological literature for years. While researching for the book, I chanced upon one of the earliest theories around grief, which was proposed by Sigmund Freud, considered the father of psychoanalysis. In 1917, he published the paper, 'Mourning and Melancholia'. In it, he talks about how loss can almost produce two different states in people—one that is known as mourning and the other that is known as melancholia. Mourning is defined as . . . **'the reaction to the loss of a loved person, or to the loss of some abstraction which has taken the place of one, such as one's country, liberty, an ideal, and so on'.**[2]

This definition really stands out for me, because even back in 1917, Freud looked upon grief and mourning not just as limited to physical death, but also connected to losses attached to objects we love. We experience mourning even in those situations. It's important to remember that the First World War was going on when Freud wrote this.

When asked about grief and its function, Kenneth Doka, a grief researcher and leading expert on grief counselling, said in an interview with Victor Yalom for Psychotherapy.net, 'I think it's probably important to acknowledge and recognize that grief is a reaction to loss. We often confuse it as a reaction to death.'[3]

Here are few examples of what clients have shared over the years with reference to loss:

Raman, a fifty-year-old man, shared in his first session, 'During the pandemic, I was fired from my job where I had worked for twenty-five years. Although it has been a year since I was asked to leave, there is a sadness that consumes me still. Being asked to leave evoked a reaction of helplessness and loss, something like what I felt when my mum passed away. I had imagined retiring from this job and had given it my all. Now, this loss has broken me. I don't know how to process it and what to do with my life.'

Sayli, a thirty-year-old woman, in therapy spoke about how hard the last few years have been. She said, 'It's been three years of trying IVF and it still hasn't worked out. With every failed attempt, my marriage is breaking apart and so am I. My husband doesn't see or understand what I'm feeling and going through. I feel so alone. He doesn't understand what my tears are for. I'm grieving for all those times when there was a possibility of us having a baby—but he can see neither my pain nor my grief.'

Minnie, a sixty-five-year-old client, mentioned, 'When I was thirty-four, a dear friend and I drifted away. That was the first time I realized that this slow fading away felt like grief and left me with a deep sadness. Before this, at various points I had experienced this feeling, but never really acknowledged and allowed myself the permission to grieve.'

These three client examples are a glimpse into how losses of various kinds evoke different degrees of grief in all of us.

Activity

Now, I want you to take a moment to think of all the times when you may have experienced loss, which evoked a feeling of grief. Write down any memories and events that come to your mind when you think of grief.

____

____

____

____

____

____

____

Here are some life events, other than the loss of a loved one to death, which can evoke a reaction of grief in us.

- A separation/divorce
- Unsuccessful attempts at trying to have a baby
- A friendship break-up
- Infidelity experienced in a relationship
- Loss of familiar structures and ways of living as experienced in the pandemic
- Ecological grief triggered by how the environment is not being cared for
- Illness and injury
- Estrangement or abandonment
- Physical or emotional neglect
- Loss of autonomy and safety

- Loss of establishments such as iconic buildings, bookstores, restaurants or music stores
- Alzheimer's disease and other forms of dementia

I have outlined these specifically as very often, these situations are not very commonly associated with grief. As a result, people experiencing these situations don't get the understanding or support they really need. As a client once articulated, 'Recognizing that my partner abandoned me has evoked a grief reaction in me. Till the time I didn't have a name for it, I couldn't make any sense of my emotions.' This insight and giving it a name allows us to embrace grief and make room for it in the various forms that it shows up. My understanding is that once we have named a feeling in therapy or to our own self, we can begin to make space for it and learn how to process the emotions, slowly and gently.

There are times where it can feel sneaky, like in a friendship, when a friend suddenly stops talking to you and you can't make sense of it. At other times, we can see it coming. Yet, in both instances, it continues to be experienced as grief—a loss that lingers.

With couples' work, often when a couple reaches out, I can sense that they are grieving a loss of the love they had for each other. At the same time, sometimes, they see therapy as the last resort. Other times, couples are deeply aware of another kind of grief that awaits them. To witness this and know that they already are in a state of anticipatory grief can be heartbreaking.

If you have experienced grief in ways that I have described above, certain chapters in this book that outline the stages of grief, the questions that we have to make peace with our loss and coping techniques, may all help you make sense of things and even find hope. At the same time, there would be questions and experiences that the book may not be able to answer, as the focus is around grief emerging from the death of a loved one.

Every time our dreams, relationships and possibilities about the future seem to be fading away, we experience helplessness and carry a sense of loss within. So, hold a space where you can be gentle and kind to yourself as feelings emerge, and loss begins to sink in. Remember, grief is about love lost.

3

The Vocabulary around Loss

This chapter is an attempt at navigating terms related to grief that we misunderstand and often use interchangeably, even though they assume different meanings. The idea is to help develop a vocabulary, a language that allows us to understand our grief and what comes with it or also offer support and presence to others who may be grieving.

Grief and Grieving

This definition by Mary Frances O'Connor, who is an associate professor at the University of Arizona and author of the book, *The Grieving Brain: The Surprising Science of How We Love and Learn from Loss,* captures the distinction between 'grief' and 'grieving' succinctly. 'Grief really is that feeling that you have, the sort of intensity that just overwhelms you, and that sort of momentary experience. Grieving, on the other hand, is the way that grief changes over time without ever actually going away.'[1]

One of the important ideas in this book is to provide an understanding of the process whereby we can hold space for our grief and grieving. By doing so, we can carry the love and loss together.

Bereavement

While the terms 'bereavement' and 'grief' are often used interchangeably, it helps to separate the two as while they may have common characteristics, they do have different meanings. In a paper titled 'Grief and Bereavement: What Psychiatrists Need to Know', published by *World Psychiatry*,[2] researchers Sidney Zisook and Katherine Shear talk about the difference. They say, 'Researchers have suggested that the term "bereavement" be used to refer to the fact of the loss; the term "grief" should then be used to describe the emotional, cognitive, functional and behavioural responses to the death.'

As discussed earlier, grief is not used only in relation to loss due to death. It is also used when we talk of the pandemic as a period of collective grief, or loss of a future and shared memories when a separation or divorce happens, or also to describe the loss experienced, for instance, when your favourite bookstore chose to close doors, leaving you with the sharp pain of loss.

The American Psychological Association (APA) says, 'Bereavement is the condition of having lost a loved one to death. Hence, the term bereaved is used in relation to the individual or family, who lost a loved one. The characteristic of loss lies at the heart of both bereavement and grief.' The APA, further mentions, 'Bereavement may also signify a change in social status (e.g., from wife to widow)—bereaved *adj*.'[3]

Onset of grief versus bereavement: While bereavement begins the moment we recognize that we have lost a loved one, for some, grief may be delayed or absent and its onset may only be sometime later. For some, both bereavement and grief may be experienced simultaneously, and their onset may be at the same time. Mayank, a twenty-nine-year-old male client, with tears in his eyes shared, 'My mum called me to say that Papa had a heart attack and had passed away. I couldn't believe what she said and had to ask her to repeat it. She asked me to come home as soon as I could. I remember booking my tickets, packing my stuff and replaying what my mum said, but I don't know if I was feeling grief. I remember thinking that I would be the first in my friends' circle to lose a parent. As soon as I saw my mum, I remember a sharp feeling of pain and helplessness. Now I know that I was experiencing grief. All the rituals, mourning helped me feel and recognize that there was so much that was overwhelming me.'

Mourning

This has to do with the way grief is expressed. Our grief and how we feel within is very private, though the fact that one is bereaved and grieving is likely known to others. Mourning has to do with an outward expression of grief. In a paper titled, 'Mourning and Grieving', Benson Mulemi spells out the definition, differences and what lies in common. He states in the paper, 'The outward social and emotional expressions of grief embody the notion of mourning. The expressions include weeping, social and religious performances in dirges and funeral rites, wistful discourse about a deceased person or entity associated with perceived loss, and ascetic actions.'[4]

We know that it is grief, which in turn leads to mourning. At the same time, mourning and associated rituals may look different across communities and religions. As a result, whether it's a funeral, prayer meeting, wake or dress code, all of them allow for mourning and simultaneously for rituals and traditions that let the grieving person make sense of it all. Sujoy, a thirty-year-old-client, who lost his brother mentioned, 'I couldn't believe that I had lost my brother. It was as if I was in denial. We decided to do an electric cremation and I stood there at the crematorium for a very long time, because that was when it sunk in that he had really gone, and I would never see him again. My best friends stayed with me. The next day, when I had to go and collect the ashes from the crematorium for immersion, the loss became more real. I knew that there was no denial. It allowed for some acceptance. While my wife was worried that all this would break me, I felt that these rituals helped me, I could make sense of death.'

In the paper, Benson Mulemi summarizes mourning by stating, 'Mourning thus encompasses the visible personal and collective expressions of grief.'

Our mourning rituals across traditions and faith allow for support and even a certain structure and predictability that helps grieving individuals and families. At the heart of all mourning rituals is a sense of community. When we are grieving, we feel alone at every level and at that time, whether we recognize or not, having relatives and friends come over and be present allows for a sense of stability. It creates a safe space for grief to be expressed. As Mary-Frances O'Connor, author of the book, *Grieving Brain,* says, 'Mourning rituals can offer constancy and comfort in a moment when everything can feel very uncertain. By connecting us to rituals that have existed for hundreds of years, we are reminded that those who came before us have experienced grief and uncertainty, and they have carried on and restored meaningful lives.'[5]

Activity

Take some moments to sit down and ask yourself what this chapter evokes for you.

____

____

____

____

Follow it up with thinking about which mourning rituals allowed you to experience community and which rituals you struggled to make sense of.

The more we understand and make sense of the vocabulary around grief, our grieving journey begins to make sense to us.

4

How Grief Shows Up

For years, when my dad was sick and between hospital visits, I wondered what grief would look like. As a child, all I knew was that it would feel extremely sad and I felt fearful thinking that I would have to face it, whenever it happened. When my dad did pass away in 2013, I was taken aback by how not just emotionally, but physically, cognitively and interpersonally, it impacted me.

To begin with, it felt unreal till the time his body was being taken for cremation. I also had low blood pressure consistently on all those days. I remember feeling extremely hungry and weak just before his cremation and wondering how others would judge me for that. I felt guilty about my hunger, which was unusual for me. I felt nauseous and dizzy for days after his loss. There was confusion and anger, which stayed for days, and the world just didn't make sense. I was the first among my friends to lose a parent and I wondered 'why me' for quite some time.

Then, ten years later, when I lost my father-in-law, I thought, 'I know what grief feels like.' But I was wrong. Grief is sneaky and we change, so how it shows up also could change. This time around, I actually had what I call 'grief fog', where I was disoriented and started forgetting things. I experienced intense emotions in waves, although my blood pressure remained absolutely fine.

The table below is a description of how grief impacts us at various levels and very often, we wonder if we are the only ones experiencing this.

Physical	Emotional	Behavioural	Interpersonal	Cognitive
Lack of appetite.	A deep yearning for the deceased.	Inability to eat, increased hunger and significant weight changes.	Avoidance when it comes to meeting people, even close friends sometimes.	Grief fog. Disruption in earlier routines and structure.
Aches and pains, change in activity levels.	Sharp sense of sadness.	Uncontrollable sobbing.	Inability to participate in social interactions.	Inability to concentrate and pay attention.
Nausea, feeling dizzy. Gut issues, chronic headaches and backaches.	Emptiness and loneliness.	Inability to get started on doing things or take initiative.	Finding conversations meaningless and hard to navigate.	Experiencing forgetfulness.
Exhaustion. Impact on libido and sex drive.	Shame and guilt.	A visible sense of tiredness.	Feeling not understood.	Changes in motivation, ambition levels.

Weight gain or weight loss.	Relief	Visible signs of how socialization and engaging take effort.	Lowered patience and stress tolerance in relationships.	Consistent feeling of dullness.
Hypersomnia/ Insomnia.	Anxiety		Change in how we perceive our intimate relationship and friendships.	Feeling disoriented in the context of day and timings.

Physical and Behavioural Symptoms

As with trauma and anxiety, grief finds a way into our body. All of us, who have experienced grief, know that there is a sense of exhaustion, both physical and emotional, that takes over. It is hard to explain. My personal experience is that it makes us feel empty and leaves us with a feeling that there is not much to give or any energy to spend. I have heard clients describe how they felt—there was no or low energy and as a result, they fainted due to shock, exhaustion and, at other times, because of not eating.

Lack of appetite and poor sleep is another symptom that clients show up with. But at the same time, there are others who experience an increase in their appetite and hypersomnia. Hypersomnia or sleeping excessively for a grieving individual is a way of shutting themselves off from reality and hoping that once they wake up, things will be different. The exhaustion is so palpable that sometimes, sleeping is all they think they can do. As a society, we often can be judgmental about people who engage in hypersomnia, forgetting that grief shows up for different individuals in different ways.

Grief also finds an outlet in psychosomatic ways: whether it's gut issues such as constipation, irritable bowel syndrome, stomach aches, headaches, back pains and skin flare-ups. Many of my clients have reported increased hair loss after losing a loved one. Others have reported feeling a consistent tension and stiffness in the body, and joint pains. Some clients feel that they are feverish physically, although they may not be running a fever. Our immunity is impacted in the light of grief and as a result, it's common for grieving individuals to fall sick and catch infections in the first few months of the loss. This can be frustrating and very tiring to an individual, who already feels like they are working with limited energy.

Difficulty breathing, chest pain and palpitations are other symptoms that clients report. Panic attacks, nightmares and frequent dreaming is also what a lot of grieving individuals experience. Sometimes, people report that they can actually feel their heart paining, and it is unbearable. The reality is that when we lose a loved one, we feel heartbroken and that heartache sometimes shows up for people in this way.

Grieving clients have talked about how they sometimes have either gone back to smoking, or their smoking has increased as they were trying to cope. Others have reported an increase in smoking weed or the urge to do drugs as they feel too overwhelmed and want to numb the pain. Patterns of binge drinking or dependence on alcohol are also mentioned by grieving individuals. Some talk about how their increased frequency of drinking or transition to daily drinking is something that bothers them, but they find it hard to stop. However, these reactions are, in my view, ineffective ways of coping. They may temporarily allow for the pain to be numbed, but in the long run they come in the way of coping. Knowing that the grieving journey is long and grief lasts, while some of these may serve as escape, they increase the possibility of the individual developing a dependency on these behaviours. These behaviours can come in the way of dealing with the grief.

Clients have talked about how it gets difficult to leave home or exercise. Then there are others, who have talked about how they took to running and working out when they found themselves dealing with crippling grief. I, too, found solace in going for long walks when I was grieving. Long solitary walks or running and being in nature helped me to centre myself and also keep coming back to the present as I struggled with grief.

Emotional and Interpersonal

Grief impacts us at multiple levels, and we often feel a multitude of emotions all at once. There are also times we may feel numb. This is a reminder that we are overwhelmed by the enormity of our feelings and as a result, our body and mind shut down.

There are times when our grief may show up in uncontrollable sobbing, shrieking with pain, longing and then silently crying in the washroom or into a pillow, with an inability to hold back tears. That's why sometimes, bereaved individuals choose to distance themselves from social situations. They don't know when their tears may emerge and what may evoke fear in them. This is what leads to social withdrawal.

Grief at an emotional level takes away our capacity for joy and it feels like all our vitality is taken away from us.

Our window for tolerance and patience threshold often gets impacted in the light of grief. When my father-in-law passed away, I realized that I found it hard to be fully present and enjoy conversations in large groups. I would feel irritated, thinking about how meaningless and empty the conversations sounded. In the presence of grief, many conversations seemed shallow. As I began to recognize this, I made a choice to not go into large group interactions when possible. When I had to, I would go with an exit plan. With friends and family, who understood, I would talk about how I was not ready to socialize.

As we make sense of the loss, we can be left feeling very raw. As a result, grieving individuals sometimes talk about how they feel easily hurt and irritated by comments that didn't really upset them as much earlier. Being aware of how grief has made us more sensitive to certain comments and statements helps us in being mindful in the ways we respond to others.

When grief strikes, all that we had assumed to be stable, safe and secure no longer feels the same. Grieving individuals describe the initial period as one where they are lost and feel completely anchorless. Everything that offered certainty seems to be shaken. Dr Colin Murray Parkes, who is a psychiatrist and author, has extensively talked about this in his books, explaining the concept of the 'assumptive world' model. Neelima, who had lost her pet dog Mr Gingerly, mentioned how all her friends have pets. The first month, she felt that she couldn't bear to go to anyone's house as it reminded her of the void in her own life.

Since grief changes our world, it's very common for clients to feel physically and psychologically unsafe and hence hypervigilant when it comes to their own well-being and that of their loved ones. Grief makes us feel helpless and we begin to recognize that our sense of control was taken away from us. That's why hypervigilance becomes a way of finding control once again. My experience is that most people who engage in it are often not aware of this. It can often show up for clients in the form of increased anxiety and fears in relation to one's own health or that of loved ones.

Makrand, who was thirty-two, lost his mother to a cardiac arrest. She was fifty-eight and extremely healthy. Ever since her loss, he would make his sister, father and wife go for medical check-ups every three months. He reached out to me six months after his mum's demise as he began to recognize that that any sign of physical ill-health, such as a headache or cold, would get him highly anxious, to the extent that he would have sleepless nights.

I have heard clients tell me that amidst grief, they feel a desire to just run away from it all. Sometimes, the grief is so intense that people don't have the energy in them to bear and deal with the pain that a loved one's death is evoking. I have worked with grieving individuals who, after the death of their loved one, have struggled with thoughts around self-harm and engaged in such behaviour. Akram lost his brother to suicide and when he began therapy, his first sentence was that he was very scared that he would harm himself. There is research that shows that in families where loved ones have been lost to suicide, the risk factor for suicide increases for family members of the deceased. If you find yourself struggling with thoughts around self-harm and suicidal ideation, it's important to reach out to a mental health professional and seek help.

For people who have lost their partner to death, marriage functions can often be a big trigger. Sunit, after losing her husband to a bike accident at the age of thirty, told me, 'It's hard to be there for my friend's wedding. It reminds me of my own grief and loneliness. Weddings are designed for couples and families and it's hard to show up and not feel sorrow. I have avoided some weddings because of this.' Our interpersonal avoidance is a function of the feeling that people don't understand us, or that our identity has only been reduced to grief and people can't see anything beyond that. This is discussed in Part 3 of the book in detail.

Our Relationship with Faith, Religion and Hope

At an emotional level, grief often changes how we feel about hope, life at large and also our relationship with spirituality, and then religion. There are people who, in the aftermath of grief, find themselves in a place of anger and rage, questioning everything—whether it's the idea of God or faith. Many find themselves struggling with nihilism. At the same time, there are others who feel that their faith and belief in a higher power and God was strengthened or born in moments of grief.

I remember working with a family, who had lost a member to suicide. The sister said, 'The chanting and prayers helped me find an anchor; I could surrender.' The brother, on the other hand, said, 'I don't know what to believe in anymore. I find myself listening to music and reading literature that's built on the principles of nihilism.'

I remember their mother telling me how she was confused and overwhelmed, not knowing what to do or how to support her two children, who had such different and opposite ways of responding to grief.

Cognitive Symptoms in the Aftermath of Loss

Grief engulfs us and it feels like we are so consumed by it that we can't see, think or even remember things clearly. That's why forgetting, difficulty in concentrating and feeling foggy-headed in the initial days of loss is very common. Our inability to focus or attend to chores are some ways in which our ability is impacted. A client told me how she would end up sleeping and forget to give her pet their food on time, and even forget to eat herself. She would feel immensely guilty and terrible for that, but felt like she couldn't do anything about it. When she reached out to me, her words were, 'I know I'm grieving, but I seem to be losing my mind. I can't remember the basic things. It's like I'm falling apart, and I no longer know what to do.'

Feeling disoriented and confused in the first few months of the loss is very common. Sometimes, it's hard to separate one day from the others. One may mix up dates, miss important ones and find it hard to be attentive and fully present. Tasks that we could do easily and found enjoyable can suddenly feel effortful and purposeless.

When the grief is traumatic, like death due to suicide or an accident, the ways in which grief is felt and experienced can be very intense. Kunal, a doctor, told me, 'I lost my wife to suicide, and while I got back to work a week after her loss, I realized that my memory was affected. During many appointments, I felt that my mind was clouded, and I began to forget my patient's detailed history; sometimes, I would even forget what they shared in their last check-up. No one ever told me that grief can impact my memory, too.'

As Kunal worked in therapy and acknowledged this, we talked about how he consciously needs to start using cues, take more detailed notes, try mnemonics and even double-check with patients when in doubt. As he continued doing the work of processing the loss, his memory started coming back. It took some months, however. Forgetfulness is one of the ways in which our grief shows up. It's more common than you think. The impact grief has on us cognitively is also referred to as 'grief brain'. I have experienced it, too, and if you are struggling with this, remember to be gentle with yourself. When I felt 'grief fog', I acknowledged it and tried to not beat myself up over experiencing it. I slowly accepted it, and as I worked towards integrating the grief, spent more time in nature, built an exercise routine and spoke to friends and family, it began to fade away over six to seven months.

Learning not to blame oneself or displacing our anger as we deal with the cognitive impact of grief is very crucial. **Mindfully working towards changing the pace at which we work, choosing monotasking over multitasking and then giving oneself more time than usual to finish tasks allows us to hold space for our own self.**

Our life and its structure often revolve around our loved ones. So, very often, people wake up and lose all their daily routines when a loved one is lost. Neelima, who lost her dog, told me, 'I don't know any more what to do with my morning. I would get up and take Mr Gingerly for a walk and then come back home, and have tea while he would sit next to me. Now, I don't go out, but I also forget to have my tea and feel that life is purposeless.' Neelima felt that her motivation, ambition and sense of purpose were lost amid her grief. She didn't know how to work or run her life. This is something that I very commonly hear from clients. This shows up in behaviours such as inability to plan, procrastination and difficulty in making small and big decisions. Neelima told me, 'I'm failing at everything, I no longer know what to choose from a menu, but I also don't know what to do with Mr Gingerly's stuff.'

Given the number of decisions that need to be made soon after a loved one's loss, it's common for bereaved individuals to talk about decision fatigue. Our capacity for initiative often gets impacted in the light of grief. Others mention how there is an increase in impulsive behaviour and acting out, and an inability to regulate their emotions. A huge part of grief work is learning to recognize this and choosing to work around it.

Having friends and family members whom you trust and who can help you with some key decisions helps. It is also a time people need to separate what needs to be acted upon immediately from what can be parked, and what needs to be scheduled for a few days later. Filtering in the context of urgency and priority is necessary. Sometimes, the grieving individual may not be able to decide on these matters and so, the support system and community can play a huge role.

I have worked with clients, who fully immerse themselves in their work, and feel that their grief gets channelized in to doing things and getting matters sorted. Some of these individuals may be at the risk of overworking, overextending themselves—it can come in the way of their interpersonal relationships.

As you process your grief, remember that grief shows up in unique ways for all of us. When I work with families, I have always found that grief looks different for each member, even though all of them may be grieving the loss of the same person. This is because of the relationship we shared with the person who passed away, our own personality, and many other factors that come into play. An awareness of how grief manifests and shows up can help. As Akram mentioned, 'Knowing that others also feel and experience grief in ways similar to me is soothing. I had begun to worry that I will never ever get out of it, and what I was experiencing was problematic. I thought I had begun to pathologize my own grief, that there was something wrong with how I was grieving.'

The culture of silence can make it hard for grieving individuals to understand the range of feelings that are emerging in them. The process of working in therapy often helps clients work through in recognizing and not underplaying these symptoms.

I hope this chapter allows you to hold space for what you are experiencing. Remember that the way in which we experience grief cognitively, emotionally, physically and interpersonally changes as we begin to work towards integrating and processing it.

5

Big, All-Consuming Feelings

What often comes in the way of defining grief is the fact that it's not just one emotion. One of the reasons we feel overwhelmed when we experience loss is because we experience multiple emotions at the same time or over the course of our grieving.

Activity

Think about a time in your life when you experienced loss. Now, write down all the emotions and feelings that were evoked as you experienced the grief.

____

____

____

____

____

Some of the emotions that generally accompany grief are:

1. **Fear:** As C.S. Lewis in his book, *A Grief Observed*, writes, 'No one ever told me that grief felt so like fear.' This is a quote that might resonate with many of us. When I dealt with my anticipatory grief, all I felt for years was a fear,

a deep paralyzing fear. Then, when my father actually passed away, there was fear again about how life would be, a fear of being left alone in the world to fend for myself and also a fear of how I would change in the aftermath of grief.

In sessions, clients have told me that when a loved one is either dying or has passed away, they find themselves consumed by a free-floating fear for no ostensible reason. At other times, the fear is very specific, with clients feeling scared to travel alone, stay alone in a house or go swimming.

2. **Anxiety:** This is an emotion that is not very often associated with grief. However, in therapy, clients reach out to address the anxiety that comes with losing a loved one.

   Sujoy, who lost his brother rather unexpectedly, told me, 'I find myself worrying about everybody's health. I'm constantly overthinking about my wife's health and I'm really anxious about my mum, who's fit and fine. I feel shaky from within—there is fear and anxiety both. I feel ashamed to say this, but I'm so worried that I can't even seem to grieve.' What clients may forget is that our grief can show up in a variety of ways and sometimes, anxiety is one such emergence. The anxiety in the light of a loved one's death shows up in people finding themselves worrying over everything and feeling that they have become both fearful and nervous as individuals. This anxiety shows up in getting overprotective about loved ones, which reflects in behaviours of control.

3. **Devastating sadness and sorrow:** 'I feel my heart is broken; there is sadness and more sadness,' Ramya, a forty-nine-year-old woman, told me after she lost

her best friend to an accident. Grief comes with hurt, sadness and sorrow. It feels like the sadness within can fill the entire room and it is heartbreaking. Most people may not even have the words to articulate what they are feeling, yet their tears, which refuse to stop, often tell the story. Even when people are in disbelief there may be tears and a sadness beginning to emerge—often a reminder that the reality of loss is setting in.

4. **Anger:** No matter how the loss has been experienced, this is an emotion that can be experienced at any stage of grief. Anger may manifest in different ways—anger towards God, towards how life has been unfair, a low threshold of tolerance towards people around and so on.

   Anger at its core is related to the feeling that some injustice has been done or meted out to us. It emerges when we feel that we have been treated unfairly or there is perceived injustice. A lot of us don't even recognize that we are expressing our grief through anger. Very often, anger can be accompanied by a sense of rage, irritation and frustration. Rage is linked to feelings of helplessness and powerlessness, which is something that grieving individuals seem to experience.

5. **Feeling of abandonment:** When the loss happens, particularly due to suicide or due to an illness, some bereaved persons feel abandoned. They feel betrayed, as if they have been left to fend for themselves. I remember Ramya mentioning to me, 'My best friend Neeru's death felt like betrayal and abandonment. I feel alone and angry. Both of us never married and were about to book a house in the hills together, so that when we grew older, we could be there for each other. I feel that she broke the vow and disappeared. What am I to do with life?'

Abandonment combined with loneliness can make the bereaved feel helpless and stuck.

6. **Longing:** There are some core feelings and emotions that are common to anyone who is grieving, no matter what the loss has been, whether it's due to death or a break-up. Our longing for our loved one is one of them. It shows up in a deep sense of yearning and missing the person who is no longer around. We miss the physical touch, the presence and even the voice. Aftab, who was fifty-seven when he lost his wife to cancer, told me, 'Often, in the middle of the night, I experience a phantom sensation, a feeling that my wife is lying next to me. I long for her physical presence and touch. I sometimes feel I will forget what her touch felt like.' This yearning is generally accompanied by sadness and a feeling of emptiness. How we deal with this yearning is also a part of how we process our grief, which we talk about in a later chapter on processing grief.
7. **Hopelessness:** In the light of grief, it's hard to hold on to hope. Particularly in the first few days and months, some grieving individuals experience hopelessness combined with despair. It can feel like there is nothing to look forward to or be happy about. I remember Kiara, a twenty-nine-year-old woman, telling me, 'Since my mum passed away, I can't even imagine what my life will look like. I thought of all my life milestones in relation to her. I don't even know if marriage means anything to me or not. If she were around, I know it would have given her joy. My career success feels meaningless as there is no one who will be excited and share this with me. All I see is her absence and this hopelessness.'

8. **Loneliness:** This is an emotion that hits us immediately when we experience grief. Even when a loved one's passing is expected, it suddenly changes our world and how seen and understood we feel. My grandmother died when she was ninety-three and we knew it was coming. We had spent time with her and were mentally trying to prepare for her demise. When she passed away, my mum felt a deep sense of loneliness. My grandmom would call her every day at 11 a.m., check on her well-being and talk to her. Towards the end, it was only for a couple of minutes as she couldn't speak much. Although my mom had support from her siblings, she still felt lonely and orphaned. It's a void that takes away our very sense of belonging and in turn, leaves us feeling very lonely. So much of our identity is about relationships and when we lose a loved one, from an interpersonal point of view, there is a loneliness that sets in, no matter how much support and love we have.
9. **Isolation:** Very often, grief is followed by a sense of isolation. For a time, it can feel like nobody understands what you are feeling and the intensity with which you are experiencing the grief. While grief is universal and each one of us go through it, how grief shows up for all of us is very specific. Many people talk about how they find it hard to speak to anyone about their grief. Even if they do, they get the impression that people don't understand it much. We will discuss this in detail in Part 3 of the book.

   For those who lose a loved one to suicide or where there were mixed feelings about the deceased, a fraught relationship or when the death happened due to drug or alcohol overdose, grieving individuals often hesitate to share, due to feelings of shame, guilt, anger or the fact that they wouldn't be understood. This in turn makes the grieving journey very lonely, where a lot is left unsaid and unaddressed.

10. **Emptiness:** 'A single person is missing for you, and the whole world is empty.' – Joan Didion, *The Year of Magical Thinking*

    Haven't we all struggled with this emptiness in the light of grief? It can make us wonder about the very purpose of living. It poses existential questions in the context of what happens to our life as we continue to live and participate in worldly affairs. Aftab told me, 'I spent three years as a caregiver for my wife, who was dealing with cancer. My day revolved around her needs, her life and I would have done it for all my life, but she died last year. Now, it all feels empty. I have nothing to do, and it feels like I lost myself, my world, everything with her. There is not much to do, and my life feels empty and lonely.'

11. **Relief:** This is one emotion associated with grief that we don't talk about enough or choose to not even mention. Relief as an emotion is what we experience when we feel a release from a situation that was distressing, threatening and even anxiety-provoking. As a result, we feel lighter, less hypervigilant and can breathe easy.

    In my work, I have seen a large number of clients experience relief when their loved one passed away, particularly if the latter were struggling with long-standing physical illnesses that were chronic and progressive or cognitive mental health conditions like dementia.

    Alisha, a thirty-five-year-old female client, mentioned, 'My mum was frail, falling apart and forgetting who all of us were. The last four years with her illness had been very hard. Every day we saw her, it felt like she was dying a little. Due to her dementia, she had even lost the capacity to speak. We didn't know how she was feeling. When she died, we all felt relief as she was in too much pain and there was nothing more that we could have done. I love her and still think of her and miss her—but seeing her die in front of my eyes everyday was the hardest part. I felt so helpless.'

Other situations that could be associated with relief are when there have been years of caregiving and a certain degree of fatigue and exhaustion have set in. Clients also talk of relief sometimes in situations when there was abuse or addiction involved. **It is important to remember that relief and deep sorrow can coexist.** If for years, you have been struggling with anticipatory grief, the death—when it actually happens—it can possibly bring relief and grief at the same time. As a result, very often, relief is accompanied by a feeling of guilt. We begin to think of ourselves as bad people, who feel relief in the aftermath of a loved one's death. The reality is that we can still love someone deeply and yet feel relief when they pass away. It is normal and a part of being human.

If you find yourself experiencing these complex emotions simultaneously, it is okay to give yourself permission to feel and talk to either loved ones who understand or seek support through a support group/ individual counselling.

12. **Shame:** There are times when grief comes accompanied with feelings of shame, combined with anger and even hatred for the person who passed away, particularly when there was addiction involved—like alcohol or drugs, for instance. Even in the case of suicide, I have worked with family members who have

felt a sharp sense of shame, as they worry that others will blame them for the actions of the deceased.

Kaizad, a twenty-eight-year-old, told me, 'My father was an alcoholic, and he would hide and drink from us. He would be a different person under the influence of alcohol. Over the years, I disconnected from him and even began to despise him for not controlling his impulse to drink. I would feel shame when guests came over or at public functions, where he would slur or drink excessively. Even after he died, I felt so much shame that I never told anyone including my own wife, whom I met a year later, about it. It's been five years since his death. This is the first time I'm talking about his alcoholism. Nobody knows and I still feel shame, it's as if I'm carrying the shame and it's a burden. I'm tired.'

13. **Guilt:** It's very common in the aftermath of loss for grieving individuals to experience guilt. Often, grieving individuals struggle with the feeling that they didn't do enough and what-if scenarios pop up in their minds (this is discussed in detail in Part 4). No matter, how the death happened, guilt often lingers. However, if the death happened due to suicide, accidents, homicide or on a holiday/trip, the guilt heightens as it is hard for people to make sense of it. Often, the surviving individual thinks about what they could have done to change it. The grieving individual is left with their own survivor's guilt. Therapy sessions are filled with heartbreaking stories of individuals who wonder and keep asking questions which are reflective of guilt they feel, such as:
    'Why did I sleep in the car? If I were awake, could I have averted the accident?'

> 'I shouldn't have left the room at all. My dad would have not fallen off the bed.'
>
> 'Why did I not accompany my brother on the trip? If I was there, things could have changed.'
>
> This guilt can be self-consuming and often comes in the way of the individual's healing.

This list of feelings evoked in the light of grief is not exhaustive and there could be many more emotions that people experience based on the relationship they shared with a loved one, the factors that surround their death and also individual grieving styles.

The intensity with which these feelings are experienced and how they show up, immediately after the loss and over time, is something that's hard to tell.

It is okay to acknowledge that some people will experience feelings very intensely and sharply, while others may feel that after a few initial days, their emotions come in waves, and they come and go.

I remember Romi, who lost her mum to a cardiac arrest suddenly, mentioned in a session, 'I always thought that I would be devastated if something happened to my mum. But a week into it, when I have accepted that nothing can be done, I'm coming to terms with the loss. My friends and relatives coming, the funeral and the memorial service all helped in making sense that it had to happen. My eyes well up when I talk and think of her and at the same time, I feel intense emotions come in waves. Sometimes, I can see them coming; other times, out of nowhere, I will be swept away by an emotion of longing. At the same time, when my colleagues came yesterday, I was surprised that I could smile; but as soon as they left, I felt exhausted and extremely lonely. It's a strange feeling—the grief feels sneaky and yet I know now that there is not much I can do.'

Grief is not just one big feeling, but the recognition that we will feel many big feelings all together and it will hurt and pain, even if we can't name the feeling. As I always tell clients, what makes trauma and grief so hard is that it can feel like the floodgates of emotions are all opened at the same time. It can feel hard to fathom what's happening. It can be overwhelming as we begin to experience various emotions altogether.

There are times when the grieving individuals can experience two opposing emotions at the same time. This will be further discussed in chapter on 'Mixed Feelings' in Part 4. The bereaved can experience relief and guilt at the same time, they can be grieving and yet feel hopeful about life. While this ambivalence can be confusing for others, it's normal for people to experience mixed feelings.

Recognizing this duality and paradoxical reality is the biggest part of making sense. If you are supporting someone who's dealing with these paradoxical emotions, learning to accept what the bereaved is saying, without trying to judge them for it, is the biggest part of grief.

Rani, a sixty-five-year-old woman, mentioned during a workshop, 'My husband was bedridden for ten years and I did everything for him. Now, I miss him a lot, I feel lonely and think about him. However, I also feel free. His death made me sad, but it was freeing, too. Two days after his death, my daughter told me how it would be hard to build a new routine and deal with emptiness. She said that still, I will finally have a chance to lead life the way I want and maybe my life will feel better. As soon as I heard this, I couldn't stop crying.'

What's important to keep in mind is that how one experiences emotions over the course of grieving continually changes. Learn to trust the process. Remember that the feelings that emerge in the aftermath of grief are layered and complicated.

6

The First Few Days

The first few days of loss is the stage where people experience acute grief. The grieving individual may experience intense feelings of loss, yearning for the deceased, melancholy, denial, disbelief, anger, guilt and anxiety. These feelings are experienced as being strong, intense and present all the time. This time can be disorienting, confusing and the hardest when it comes to making sense. The first week or the first month may feel like a blur. This is the time when grief impacts us physically, emotionally and cognitively all at once. We may feel disoriented, unable to eat or sleep, cry inconsolably and have consistent, repeated thoughts about the person who died. We may also find ourselves struggling with feelings of helplessness and hopelessness and unable to imagine a future. This is also a time where it feels like there is no way out and we feel that we will never be able to deal with the loss. We may find ourselves stuck in a palace of despair and feel that life has lost all meaning.

There is no way to make it easier and yet, I can tell you that people stay with the pain, sorrow and slowly they begin to come to terms with it. I remember one person asking me, 'Does it ever get easier?' My answer to her and I still believe it, was that it would always hurt, and we will continue to miss the person, but as we begin to accept and make sense of things, we begin to live our life and hold the grief, too.

Here are some possible pointers that can help in the early days:

1. **Choose yourself:** I often remind clients that answering emails and messages can wait. Everybody understands that they are grieving, and they don't need to get back into normal life right away. This is not the time when one needs to fall for 'should' and 'must'. This is the time to pause and be present for yourself and loved ones who need you.
2. **Wait out on big decisions:** One of my insights from my client work and dealing with grief is about learning to pause and park big decisions. Grief can be debilitating and decisions that are made in the first week or month are often compromised, as the grieving person may feel overwhelming emotions. I generally tell clients that it's okay to take time about making big decisions, such as moving house, dealing with finances or even emptying and clearing the deceased's cupboard. During this time, it can feel like you are consumed with emotions that are hard to process. On top of this, to burden yourself with big decisions that can have long-term consequences is not a good idea. For instance, in the early days of grief, even when someone asks, 'What can I do for you?', it feels hard to articulate or even ask for anything, because one feels so much sorrow. It's a time where nothing really makes sense. Taking any big decision, that will have lasting consequences in such a time is not a good idea. Allow yourself at least the first fifteen days to a month to make sense of what's happening.

   I remember Rishabh, a twenty-eight-year-old man, lost his wife in an accident when she was travelling in a different city. They had been married for two years and had moved into a new house. Richa, his wife was walking on the pavement and a car suddenly came on to the pavement out of nowhere and hit her. He told me, 'The family insisted that I should clear my wife's cupboard when they were around in the first week of her death itself. I was in no state to decide and I couldn't say no. But I felt like they violated my right to do it when I was ready. While they came from a good place, the reality is that I began to resent them. I felt like a robot; I couldn't get myself to decide and hence, they chose for me, which seemed unfair. The thought of sorting through her stuff got me so anxious, I was not ready to step into our bedroom. I didn't sleep that night and I told them that I was not ready to do it yet.'

Grief is exhausting and when we burden ourselves with the big tasks, we exhaust ourselves further.

3. **Understand the role of friends and family:** I have on occasion worked with clients where they don't have the option to wait things out and, in those situations, grief can often worsen. The role of friends and family in such moments is crucial. Naren, a fifty-five-year-old man, said, 'I was too busy to process what was really happening. I did cry at the funeral and on the day when I heard about my father's fatal heart attack. But there was so much to do that my brain was overwhelmed with logistics. I was extremely calm as I knew that no one else would be able to arrange for the various rituals and prayer ceremony. I remember my partner telling me that she was worried that I was suppressing my emotions, but the reality was that there was no time or space in which I could give myself permission to grieve. I had to sort through his stuff in those early days as I was

moving away to join a new job and had already delayed my joining for two weeks. It helped that my wife and my dad's friend were around when I had to sort through the stuff.' So, leaning on support and asking for help is important. Make room for it.

4. **Structure:** I know how hard this sounds, but having a basic structure can be of great use in the first few days of loss. **All that structure needs to include is having your meals, choosing to take a bath and trying to get rest whenever possible**. Each of these tasks by itself can feel like an effort and sometimes, you may not even realize that you have missed having your meal or taking a bath. Mira had lost her mum in an accident when she was four years old and her father passed away when she was thirty-three. She started sessions two months after her father's death and mentioned 'All I did was cry and sleep for the last entire few months. My best friend flew down from Mumbai and she saw to it that I ate my meals, she insisted I go for a shower and just sat with me holding my hand, all throughout the first week. If not for her, I would have fallen sick and I don't know how I would have survived.'

   If you are a family member supporting someone who is grieving, try and be gentle as you help them with structure. Remember that for the person grieving, nothing makes sense. For them, some of the simplest tasks are the hardest to do. Choose to be physically present—it's a huge support and even the very basic acts such as getting them food on a plate, helping them get ready to go for a shower or just being in the room as they try to fall asleep can help.

5. **Be receptive to help and ask for help:** If you are grieving, allow yourself to be supported and recognize

that experiencing vulnerability is not a sign of weakness. Choose to recognize the intensity of grief and don't underestimate its effect on you. If you want a family member or friend to stay, ask for it. If they offer that on their own, accept it. You need it—being alone at that point is not what you require.

6. **Surround yourself with people who understand:** Tanuja, who is forty-eight, told me, 'While I was grieving, I realized how some relatives can be so demanding. In our family, food is not cooked in the house till the funeral takes place. So, my friends sent over food. By the second day, our family from different cities showed up. While most of them were supportive and understanding, I had a few close relatives behave in such insensitive ways that I felt hurt and betrayed. Since we had so many kin over, my daughter organized food from outside as no one was in a state to cook and plan. My husband's brother began complaining about how the salt was less in the food and how he preferred homemade food. I didn't know what to say, but I quietly ate. When they asked me if they should stay for few more days and if I needed help, I told them that I would manage. Isn't it strange that even in moments of grief, people expect you to be the perfect host? I wonder how people with the best intentions can still be so cruel.'

   Therapy sessions are filled with stories where clients have talked about how relatives, family members and even friends have made remarks that have felt cruel and inappropriate in the context of a death that has just happened. I would still like to give the benefit of the doubt to these family members, who may not even be aware of what they are doing. At the same time, as a therapist, I'm aware of and recognize how frustrating it can be for the bereaved individual to be at the receiving end of these comments and demands.

Here is the thing: you would not really know how relatives and family members will react till the loss happens. There is no way to prepare for this situation, but it helps to allow yourself to acknowledge the emotion and unpleasant sensations that their behaviour evokes in you, in those moments.

I remember discussing this with a friend when I found myself in this situation, and she said, 'When a loved one dies, you see all kinds of people—some who are actors, some who want drama and some who never showed up or were there for you before, but now behave as if they are really close to you.'

Whether you like it or not, there are certain people activated only in the aftermath of grief. Claire, who is sixty-eight, shared in the session, 'My brother was bedridden for months and on dialysis. We knew he only had a few days to live. His health was deteriorating, and his best friends and our other sister didn't visit him much. While he was unwell, he would talk about how everybody seemed to have forgotten him and how lonely he felt. When he died, all of them came and talked about the impact he had on their life, and they kept crying. I felt like I was part of a soap opera, where they were pretending to be close. However, their actions in the months preceding his death and after the death itself never added up. I wished that they had chosen to tell him what they told me. Also, after the burial, all of them disappeared. All they did a little later was drop a message and ask if I needed help with financial stuff. I was left to live in an empty house, when after the ceremonies were done, what I needed was presence and social support. I wonder if people create an illusion of closeness when others are watching and then believe that a WhatsApp message is enough. It would have helped if they came occasionally. I didn't need help with logistics, but I hated being alone.'

7. **Dealing with exhaustion:** The first few days can feel back-breaking. The crying, the logistics around organizing the funeral/cremation, meeting guests and well-wishers who visit, can all come with fatigue that you have never felt before. Most people I have worked with and known underestimate this exhaustion and don't allow themselves an opportunity to fully embrace how the fatigue has set in. I can tell you that the body carries the score. I remember thinking that if I began working slowly, I would be able to cope better. In the days following grief, it's okay to not be productive and not to preoccupy oneself with work. If your workplace provides bereavement leave, make a choice to use it.

    Grief can feel very confusing in the initial few days and months. On one day, you will feel like you have accepted and are coping with the loss. The next day, suddenly, it feels like grief has come back and the tears refuse to stop. Choosing to recognize the messy and unpredictable nature of grief is one of the ways we allow ourselves to rest. When it comes to therapy sessions, for the first few months, I generally tell clients that we choose to stay with what they are feeling, and not rush in to believing that they have accepted or integrated the loss. Each day looks different and each session may bring either insights that offer hope or overwhelming emotions.

> The first few days can feel unbearably lonely and filled with despair, so choose to be gentle and not pathologize your grief.
>
> For some folks, the grief doesn't completely sink in during the initial few days as they are filled with rituals and guests. It's the to-do list and logistical necessities that take precedence. For them, the grief begins to sink in a few days after the rituals are done, when the guests have left. I remember when my dad passed away, my grandmother mentioned this to us and said that she would stay back. Her quiet, supportive presence helped when my mum found herself flooded with overwhelming emotions in the first month. The advice helped us be more realistic as a family about the course that grief takes.

Remember that the first few days are extremely hard, and it can feel like we will never be able to live again and experience any emotion other than loss. I can tell you that by the time you begin to do the inner work and process the grief, you slowly start repurposing your life—although it remains hard and the void lingers.

7

Models of Grief

Given that grief shows up in different ways for different people, the theories that have evolved over the years have tried to explain different facets of how death impacts us and changes us, as also how we deal with it. For those of us who are cerebral beings, we often use theories and models to make sense of what we are feeling. These models provide an outline and describe how people navigate grief in general. Some of my clients have mentioned to me that understanding these theories has helped them feel that they are not alone as they process their emotions. Some of them have found solace as they find a certain vocabulary that helps them make sense of their own grief.

While there are many theories available around grief, I have decided to focus on only a few of them.

Elisabeth Kübler-Ross Theory

'You will not "get over" the loss of a loved one; you will learn to live with it. You will heal and you will rebuild yourself around the loss you have suffered. You will be whole again, but you will never be the same. Nor should you be the same, nor would you want to.'

—Dr Elisabeth Kübler-Ross

Dr Elisabeth Kübler-Ross was a Swiss-American psychiatrist, and her work with terminally ill individuals has substantially shaped our understanding of death and the grieving process. She is also the author of several books, including *On Death and Dying,* which was an international bestseller. Her work continues to remain relevant over the years and has allowed people to talk about death, imminent death and what it evokes in them. This was at a time when the topic was considered a taboo, and her pioneering work helped not just build a vocabulary around grief but also allowed for building a space of empathy and understanding for the terminally ill individuals and their caregivers.

It is her work with terminally ill clients that led her to describe the five stages of dying in *On Death and Dying* (1969). Then, almost three decades later, she and David Kessler, who is considered an authority on grief, co-authored a book called, *Grief and Grieving: Finding the Meaning of Grief through the Five Stages of Loss,* where she adapted these stages in the context of grief.

They talk about how the stages are part of a framework, and help people identify what they may be feeling. At the same time, they talk about how the stages are non-linear and that people don't go through them in a set order. The stages are just a way of describing what is evoked in the grieving person, in the hope that this understanding would help them navigate life in the aftermath of loss.

The stages, in their view, are:

Denial: This is a stage of grief where you know that the loss has happened, but you can't get yourself to believe it and it still feels like a dream. When we experience denial, after hearing about a loss or witnessing it, we may be in a state of shock, disbelief and may even feel numb. Numbness and feeling paralyzed in times when we are overwhelmed and consumed with emotions is our body's and mind's way of processing the shocking information.

Rita, a sixty-five-year-old client in therapy, told me, 'I came back from my morning walk as usual and as I entered the house, I realized that my husband had not woken up although it was 8 a.m. It was very unlike him. When I approached him and tried to call out, he didn't respond. In a panic, I called up my neighbours and the family doctor. The family doctor said that he had passed away in his sleep. I did hear what the doctor said, but it's as if it didn't register. I had to sit down. The news felt heavy and unbearable. I kept feeling that he would wake up now and have tea with me. I called my children, who are abroad, and told them that I didn't understand what was happening. They had to rush back as their father was no more. When my children came, my grief poured out and my tears wouldn't stop. Then, when we were taking him to the funeral, it really hit me that he was gone—I was shattered.'

Denial offers us a chance at beginning to process and absorb the enormity of a big loss. It allows us to get there slowly and begin the process of acknowledging that it has happened. What's important to remember is that it is a defence mechanism and very often, one of the first ways our body and mind responds when presented with a loss that feels life-altering. It allows people time and a window to pace the overwhelmingly strong feelings. As Ross and Kessler put it, 'There is a grace in denial. It's nature's way of letting in only as much as we can handle.'[1]

Anger: Three months after losing her husband, when Rita reached out to me for therapy, she mentioned, 'What do I feel the most? I feel rage and this deep anger towards my husband, God and everyone else. I'm angry at my husband for abandoning me and leaving me behind in this world. I also keep asking God what I did to deserve this. Why me? I no longer smile like I used to. Little things make me angry. I want answers!'

As Dr Ross had mentioned, the stages are not linear and we can feel them in any order. While Rita had begun to make sense of her life without her husband and built a new structure, the anger would keep resurfacing for her and it was the reason she began therapy.

Our anger is a reflection of our deep pain and loss. It is also a reflection of the loneliness that we experience when we are left without an anchor or someone we can rely on. Feelings of anger often come from a space where we feel that we didn't deserve this loss and grief. Very often, family members and friends of the bereaved may struggle to understand the space from where this anger is emanating, and may often say things that are not helpful or dismissive of what the bereaved individual is feeling. There are also occasions when the bereaved individual may feel angry at themselves and their own decision-making, and end up blaming themselves.

All our emotions serve as a compass and even our anger in moments of grief is trying to tell us something. Learning to acknowledge the anger and giving oneself the permission to grieve and be angry is crucial. As clients begin to do this and articulate what they are feeling, including anger, the feelings that lie underneath their anger begin to unfold and other emotions that accompany anger begin to resurface. As Rita began talking about her anger, her feelings of loneliness, emptiness and loss of safety began to emerge. It suddenly felt like anger was the tip of the iceberg and one had to create a safe space for anger before other feelings could find a way.

This understanding has often helped me to address the layers of grief as they unfold as also to address the anger, particularly when it's displaced. Displacement is a defence mechanism that individuals often end up using unconsciously to tackle certain emotions that they find unacceptable or hard to deal with. So, an individual may redirect the negative emotion they are experiencing and transfer it to another, without even realizing it. This could be a treating physician, a therapist, a psychiatrist, a caregiver or a family member who's trying to support them. While working with family members and grieving individuals, I focus on not just how and where anger finds its way, but also become aware of the ways they can acknowledge it and yet choose to hold a space for others who are trying to support them.

Bargaining: This is a stage that is filled with 'what if' and 'if only'. Bargaining is part and parcel of our life. Rita told me that she would 'always ask for the well-being of her husband and kids', and when they would be unwell, she would tell God, 'let me be sick but make them well'. Rita told me that in the first month after her husband's demise, 'I would keep praying to God to please send him back or please take me away, too.'

Remember that it's a non-linear model—Rita was dealing with denial and then bargaining. Her anger came in only three months after the loss.

Bargaining is our way of making sense of things. It is our frail attempt at hope, trying to convince ourselves that things can change, and our loved one can come back. It's a step that makes us feel less helpless as we think of various what-ifs. This has been discussed in detail in Part 4 of the book.

Bargaining is often accompanied by a sense of guilt and regret. Rita kept telling me, 'Maybe we missed something during the health examination. I wish we had started doing the health check-up twice a year and visited our family doctor every month. I shouldn't have been that careless.' The truth was that Rita had not been careless and their check-ups had happened regularly. In fact, their family doctor had even mentioned that there was no reason to believe that her husband was unwell.

In cases where there was death by accident or suicide, bargaining can last for long and take the form of self-blame, too. Often, bargaining comes with emotions of sadness, anger and disbelief, where clients mention how it's hard for them to believe what's happening. They think what's happening to them is a nightmare that will end soon, and their loved one will be back.

Our attempts at bargaining are not just in relation to God or a higher power, but also in the way we think. All the what-ifs we construe begin to show up in ruminative thoughts, where the same thought continues to run in our head—about how if we would have taken a different set of actions, the death could have been averted or avoided.

Depression: What transpires in the light of loss is a state of sadness so intense that it qualifies as a dark space in which people find themselves broken and lost, and feel depressed. The intensity and frequency with which these feelings emerge and consume us does feel like depression. This is a time when people find it hard to get out of bed, even remember what time or date it is, forget to eat or overeat and so on. Some may find themselves sleeping all day long and then there are others who are unable to sleep. This is also a time when despair takes over and grieving individuals experience both helplessness and hopelessness, which makes it so hard to be present in the moment and to imagine a future. For everyone who has experienced this state, we do know that it can feel like a stage of our life when we think we are trapped and there is no getting out of it. It feels like there is no light and there never will be. As grieving individuals struggle with this, there is huge pressure on them from family members and loved ones to get out of it and deal with it. The reality is that people take their own time; learning not to judge or pathologize too quickly what a grieving individual is going through is crucial.

Dr Kübler-Ross in *Grief and Grieving* makes the distinction about how the depression that she describes in the context of grief should not be looked upon as a symptom of mental illness. She talks about how in the presence of the loss that has happened, our feelings of depression are an appropriate response.

This is an important lens to begin with, because in its absence, there can be a hasty tendency in physicians and therapists to label clients, pathologize a normal process and introduce medication prematurely. In the next section, we will focus on grief and depression and talk about context where medication may be required. Dr Kübler-Ross also acknowledges that there are certain scenarios where the grieving individual may require medication along with psychotherapy.

Dr Kübler-Ross, while addressing the depression, draws up a beautiful metaphor that is a reminder of her wisdom and how she brought sensitivity, hope and even beauty into grief work. She says, 'As tough as it is, depression can be dealt with in a paradoxical way. See it as a visitor, perhaps an unwelcome one, but one who is visiting whether you like it or not. Make a place for your guest. Invite your depression to pull up a chair with you in front of the fire and sit with it, without looking for a way to escape.'[2]

Acceptance: This is the stage which is really misunderstood and maybe it has to do with how we as human beings generally interpret the word 'acceptance'. Acceptance is generally perceived as reaching a stage where everything feels okay, and one has fully understood and made sense of the loss. However, the reality is that with grief, the pain and longing always last. We don't reach a stage where everything feels the same. The reality is that it never will be the same. Acceptance, as Kübler-Ross saw it and as it shows up, has to do with accepting that our world has changed and will never go back to being the place it used to be when our loved one was around. It also includes acknowledging the finality of loss, embracing that they are not coming back and that we still need to find a new way to live and go on with our life. The journey leading up to this point of acceptance is a very difficult one, and it is hard. Acceptance involves acknowledging and giving ourselves permission to feel that grief will always hurt, and it will never be easy without our loved one. Sometimes, this journey into acceptance can take months and then years. At the same time, it is not easy to predict when and how grieving individuals will reach this stage.

Based on my work and my personal experience, I can tell you we reach a point where we can feel it in our bones and intuitively know that we have come to terms with and accepted the loss. It is important to understand that even when we have reached a stage of acceptance, we continue to do the work of making sense of 'who we are in the wake of the loss' and also 'the new world and how to live in it'. Simultaneously, we continue to remember, think about, and hold fond memories of our loved one and keep figuring out ways to keep the bond going, while repurposing our life—which is not easy. Six months into our session, Rita told me, 'You know, finally I stopped setting a plate for him at the dinner table. Now, I don't wake up feeling like he's lying next to me. I know he is not coming back, and I need to accept it. I can't just remain angry, passive and in denial. I hate it, but I have to find out what the world has in store for me and who I am without him.'

Meaning: This is a stage that was added by David Kessler in his book, *Finding Meaning: The Sixth Stage of Grief,* where he talks about meaning-making, and addresses different facets of finding meaning and how this impacts our acceptance and grief integration. To him, this search for meaning, irrespective of how the loss happened, was telling us about a facet of grief that needed attention.

That's why he introduced a sixth stage to grief work, which is the process of 'finding meaning', which he believes is at the core of the healing journey. In the book, David Kessler says, 'In the sixth stage, we acknowledge that although for most of us, grief will lessen in intensity over time, it will never end. But if we allow ourselves to move fully into this crucial and profound sixth stage—meaning—it will allow us to transform grief into something else, something rich and fulfilling.'[3] As he further adds, 'But finding meaning in loss empowers us to find a path forward.'

Rita, two years after the loss of her husband, told me during one of our sessions, 'I do feel some sense of peace. It's strange, but I feel that my husband dying so suddenly had some meaning to it. You know how much I hate financial stuff and administrative chores; he did all of that for us always. He wanted me to become independent, which I never was, when he was around, I hope he's smiling in heaven. If he wanted me to get my hands dirty with paperwork and administrative chores, he has been successful.'

How and when we find meaning is a very personal process and the journey towards it looks so different to each one. Knowing the human mind, sometimes our acceptance and meaning-making go hand-in-hand. As people begin to make meaning, they begin to accept the loss and it feels integrated in some way. Meaning-making can look like learning how to build a good life for yourself. At other times, it can look like devoting yourself to a cause; for some it also means acknowledging that things happen and there may not be any complete answers. Sometimes, meaning-making looks like how we keep the goodness and cherished qualities of the bereaved alive through our own life. Meaning-making is personal and it has to make sense to you—that's what is important.

People, who have lost their loved ones to addiction, rash driving, violence or mental health concerns, often turn their life's mission into spreading awareness about these concerns. This becomes a meaning-making process, whereby they find themselves continuing to heal and do the work that allows them to continue the bond with their loved one in a way.

Kübler-Ross's theory, while the most popular, has been criticized over the years. One of the biggest criticisms is that the basis of the theory is her experience of working with dying individuals, rather than bereaved individuals. What is crucial to remember though is that her stages do point to a wide spectrum of feelings that grieving individuals and their family may go through.

In addition to her theory, there are other theories that have contributed to our understanding of grief. Theories around grief began as early as 1915, with Sigmund Freud's work in which he spoke about the difference between mourning and melancholia.[4] In fact, he was the one who talked about how mourning is a normal part of loss, and we don't need to pathologize it.

Another theory that has been influential in shaping our understanding of grief is John Bowlby and Dr Colin Murray Parkes's theory, where they talked about the phases of grief as follows:

- Shock and numbness
- Yearning and searching
- Disorganization and despair
- Reorganization and repair

John Bowlby's contribution is significant as he describes how loss is so linked to our attachment. He described attachment as a 'lasting psychological connectedness between human beings'. With loss, we lose this connectedness and hence, we see the process of shock, yearning, despair and then a stage where we begin to consciously reorganize our life and start doing the work of repair.

Another popular theory is the dual process model, which was extensively researched and proposed by Margaret Stroebe and Henk Schut in 1999. The authors describe this as a model focused on coping, which they say 'refers to processes, strategies or styles of managing (reducing, mastering, tolerating) the situation in which bereavement places the individual'.

This theory builds a strong case for the fact that people oscillate between loss-oriented stressors and restoration-oriented stressors. This oscillation is a normal part of coping with grief. Loss-oriented stressors could be around doing the grief work and addressing the feelings that come with grief; restoration-oriented stressors are about how one adapts and adjusts to a new life, changes and new roles.

One of the other popular frameworks is 'The Four Tasks of Mourning' which was outlined by psychologist William Worden in his book, *Grief Counselling and Grief Therapy: A Handbook for the Mental Practitioner,* published in 1992.

According to this model, the four tasks of mourning are:

1. Accepting the reality of the loss
2. Experiencing the pain of grief
3. Adjusting to an environment with the deceased missing
4. Finding an enduring connection with the deceased, while embarking on a new life

Worden doesn't look at these as stages at all. He looks at them as processes and tasks that grieving individuals move back and forth between. He believes these tasks are not linear. What is insightful about this framework is his understanding and explanations around how the path of grief integration requires us to find a way to continue our bond with the deceased, and at the same time actively work towards building and reimagining a new life.

I remember working with Dhiraj, a fifty-eight-year-old man, who lost his wife to a lung disease. I remember that his first few words to me were, 'It's been two years and I have continued to feel grief in various ways, sometimes, anger, at other times sorrow and then sheer helplessness. I don't think I have fully come to terms with the acceptance and while I have reconstructed a new life, I don't know what to do with the memories of my wife. Should I forget and move on as everyone tells me, or is there another way? I'm really confused. My kids are surprised I'm in therapy, because they feel I have adapted well and built an almost new life, but, I still struggle.'

Dhiraj and I worked in therapy for over three years. We spent time talking about various theories of grief and models. It was Worden's theory that made the most sense to him. We talked about how it is normal to have built what feels like an almost new life and yet feel that the acceptance of loss is ongoing. Eventually, we also worked through the lens of what it would mean to embark on new paths and yet keep memories of his wife alive. I remember in one session, Dhiraj told me, 'I think talking about her in therapy and coming to you is a way of keeping her alive and reminiscing about how she brought joy to me. I like this space because it feels like every week, I can celebrate how she beautifully contributed to my life. I have decided that even when I stop therapy, I will allow myself the permission to think about her, when I wear a shirt she got me or visit a new country. I can still think about her, allow myself to feel the positive feelings that emerge when I think of her and continue my life.'

We both smiled and knew that the task of finding an enduring connection had unfolded in its own time, with the client choosing to make space for it. While working with Dhiraj, I recognized that we kept moving among the four stages and it was a reminder that the work of healing is that of a lifetime. As people begin to process grief, the intensity of pain attached to moving among these tasks reduces. As work continues to happen, there is a lightness and trust that begins to settle in for the client, even though they keep going back to the older tasks.

Another theory that has emerged in recent years is Robert Neimeyer's meaning-reconstruction theory. In a paper titled,

'GriefTherapy and Reconstruction of Memory: From Principles to Practice', Robert A Neimeyer and others say, 'Viewed from a constructivist perspective, grieving is a process of reconstructing a world of meaning that has been challenged by loss.'[5]

Robert Neimeyer talks about the three Rs of processing grief—retelling, rebuilding our bond with the loved one and reinventing our own life. He says, 'How we move towards reconstructing a bond, rather than relinquishing it, maybe lies at the heart of grief work.'

This theory makes an active case for how passing time cannot help us just address or deal with loss. What does help is an intention and action towards reconstructing and reimagining our life and in turn, our world.

While working with clients and family members, what I have learnt is that just like trauma, there will be retelling of stories, moving back and forth between experiencing distress, pain of loss and acceptance. Some of these theories can provide a scaffolding, a structure to understand how grief is experienced and for some of you, it may help to make sense. At the same time, learning to be mindful of theories, carrying them gently and not getting overly attached to any one of them is crucial. As you continue processing your grief, you may find resonance in different theories and perspectives. Yet, if these theories feel overwhelming and complicate your process, you can choose to park this and not delve into it.

Part 2

Forms of Grief

8

There Is No Hierarchy

Milli, a forty-eight-year-old client of mine, lost her completely healthy seventy-eight-year-old mother to Covid. She told me, 'I don't feel people see my grief; they think that my mum had lived enough. I feel my mum had another ten years in her. My granddad and grandmom all passed away in their mid-nineties and were completely healthy, and so was my mum. People seem to forget that grief hurts because of how much we love the person. The fact that they are ageing doesn't mean that we stop loving them and it starts hurting less. People who lost their businesses, livelihoods, their loved ones or even those who made it but spent time in hospitals recovering for days—all of us are grieving and I don't know why we turned a time of crisis into a game of, "Who is in more pain?".'

The reality is that pain is pain, and it shouldn't be put in categories or boxes or unsaid hierarchies, which is what society sometimes does. In fact, without being made explicit, there seems to be an unsaid but implicit understanding that some losses are more terrible or worse than others. For example, the loss of a child is often put at the top of the list and the loss of a pet is at the bottom. Often, the death of a younger person is looked at as being worse than that of an older one. That's why age sometimes becomes a way of invalidating the pain that someone may be going through.

A close friend's grandmother died when she was eighty-five. I remember a relative during the prayer meet telling her, 'You should remember that your grandmom lived a full life and at least she didn't suffer like so many others.' It was well-intentioned, but equally a way of trying to minimize the loss somewhat unthoughtfully.

Unconsciously, in the process of wanting to help the bereaved feel better, people make comparisons that try to drive home that their loss is not so bad. However, this very act can come across as insulting and diluting the pain of the bereaved. People in these moments forget that there is no hierarchy to grief. Every loss hurts and no matter at what age and stage of life it happens. My friend was shocked hearing that comment and, in fact, retorted saying, 'I was raised by my grandmom and I always lived with her. You are forgetting that I feel like an orphan.'

We also create hierarchies when we talk about people in the context of 'good versus bad'. We often wonder and discuss why someone who was 'such a good person' had to die so early. When someone who was regarded as a good human being passes away unexpectedly, people speak about it in the context of, 'Why do bad things happen to good people?'.

As Brené Brown in her book, *Atlas of the Heart*, says, 'Love is the last thing we need to ration in this world. But fear and scarcity trigger comparison and even pain and hurt are not immune to being assessed and ranked. Because Covid unleashed such massive fear and anxiety, we saw comparative suffering everywhere.'[1] She goes on to give examples of people comparing their losses to each other and without even realizing, engaging in a process of comparative suffering. Reading this was a reminder of what I had written in a column for *Mint Lounge* about how there is no hierarchy to grief. Grief is grief. We shouldn't downplay our own or other people's losses. Doing this is to not be empathetic or fully present to another's experience. This hierarchy of grief makes it seem like some losses aren't worth grieving for.

Imposing a hierarchy on losses robs people of their personal experience and it invalidates their suffering.

We as human beings have the capacity for love, understanding and seeing people's pain for what it is. When we find others or ourselves engaging in this pattern of comparative suffering or imposing hierarchies, we need to gently take a step back and remember that all pain deserves empathy and witnessing. Life is not a business of ranking people's pain and grief; every loss hurts and as a result, no matter what your loss is, you do have a right to talk about it and grieve for it. At the same time, honour other people's journeys and the fact that you may not understand what a loss meant to them, even as you know that they are in pain.

9

What If My Loved One Dies?

Is it normal for me to worry about my parents' death even when they are doing well?

Anticipatory grief is a state that begins even before the loss happens, where we begin to worry about our loved ones' mortality and what it will do to us, our world, and our own life. This anticipatory grief can leave us feeling scared, fearful and panicky. We wonder if our lives will be devastated because of the loss.

Here's a little truth: We have all experienced anticipatory grief.

I don't know anyone who hasn't gone through this. People may not know the term but would have experienced it. The sheer dread and helplessness that it evokes in us can be visceral. Sometimes, children as young as eight or ten years have told me how they enter their parents' room in the night to see if they are breathing properly. Both children and adults across age groups, even when their parents are healthy, have talked about this fear in sessions. They often feel guilty when they bring this up. Older folks often mention it in relation to the fear of loss of their partner, friends and talking about how it would leave them feeling lonely and their life meaningless.

The very act of sharing it in therapy takes tremendous courage and clients across age groups are teary-eyed when they share their fear and anxieties around losing a loved one.

Anticipatory grief comes up in a lot of therapy sessions, and while the clients may not often have the terminology for this, they feel the fear in their bones and know that it is unnerving. In fact, most clients tell me how they haven't shared this or ever articulated it to anyone before. We don't acknowledge it sometimes because we feel guilty that we are thinking about our loved one's demise even when they are healthy.

Sometimes, hearing about other people's loss reminds us of our own anticipatory grief. I remember when my father-in-law passed away, my clients asked me about my well-being after I resumed work. A few told me that when I had informed and texted them about my father-in-law's death, they had begun to think about how they would cope and deal with things, if their own parent or loved one passed away.

Amit, a client who just turned forty, mentioned, 'Turning forty is great and feels like a milestone. But the first thing that struck me at midnight was that I don't know if my parents will be around for the next few birthdays. As this thought hit me, I began to experience a panic attack. I started sweating and found myself gasping for breath. I got up and went through all their medical insurance papers and the next day, called my agent to increase their insurance cover. Till I did that, I couldn't feel calm and settled.'

Our own birthday can sometimes be a reminder of others' mortality, isn't it?

Earlier in the book, I have spoken about how as a child, I lived with anticipatory grief over the years, without even knowing that there was a term for it. It became a part of my life, a fear that just stayed.

I remember as my father's health deteriorated every year, I would wonder on each birthday for how long he would be around; when I had a daughter, I would think about how many of her birthdays he would get to see and be with us.

Now, in hindsight, I know that feeling grief was about the impending loss, but also the fear that his presence and love wouldn't be around. While we as human beings are great at imagining and visualizing things, we are terrible when it comes to grief. The reality is that there is no way to know, even if we try hard. The pressure we put on ourselves reflects our own anxieties, perhaps an illusion and our need for perceived control. We believe that if we know how and what we feel, we will deal with it better. As I mentioned in a column, 'This grief at its core is an existential dilemma, where we start to realize how so much in life is beyond our control.'[1]

This realization is deeply linked to the feeling, an existential truth, that we will eventually be on our own. When my father died, I realized that all the anticipatory anxiety and fears I had held for almost twenty-five years didn't really help. I had to deal with grief in a new way, and it was still hard.

Anticipatory Grief in Relation to One's Parents

Both anxiety and guilt accompany anticipatory grief. People often feel that they haven't done enough and begin to think about time being limited, with so little that can be done. For some, this may start showing up as getting obsessive about their parents' health, being hypervigilant and then feeling a continual fear that the parent(s) may not be around for too long. Amit mentioned how he would, on some nights, just enter his dad's room and check if he was breathing alright. When his father had a health issue, his anticipatory grief heightened.

There are also those who feel that this is the time they need to redeem their relationship and figure out a way to spend the most time with their parent(s). During the pandemic, a lot of my clients made a choice to return to their hometown as fears of anticipatory grief heightened, and they felt that they would carry regret in their hearts if they didn't make a conscious decision to be near their parents. The pandemic was also a time when I heard children talk about these fears all the time.

For those children, who have witnessed suicide or the deaths of their loved one very early, they sometimes begin to carry anticipatory grief as they worry that another loved one may also take their own life, or something bad would happen to them.

For those who have struggled with a difficult relationship with their parent(s), either in relation to trauma, neglect or judgement from them, anticipatory grief can come with feelings of resentment, anger, rage and a realization that they will never be seen in ways that they want. This realization can leave people shaken, sometimes angrier and at the same time deeply sad. To them, it may feel that while a parent's end is near, they are still left with open wounds. There is a sense of loss, thinking about how now there is no time left and hence, no opportunity to develop a loving relationship that a part of them still hopes for. This can be a very difficult space to be in, and if you had a complicated, ambivalent relationship with your parent, you are more likely to feel a sense of anxiety, tinged with sadness and even rage over your unmet needs. We have discussed ambivalent feelings in the fourth part of the book.

A good idea is to make space for the feelings that emerge when anticipatory grief begins to creep in. We need to remember that it's normal for all of us to feel the grief—it's a reflection of our attachment to loved ones, hence sparking fear.

At the core of our anticipatory grief is a lingering fear that once our loved one passes away, there will be a loss of self, or loss of parts of our own life that no one else knows about. There is also the loss of being seen, touched and loved in a certain way, which can never be substituted.

With grief, we lose the gaze of a loved one and know that no one will see or understand us in the same way that was soothing for us, and defining of who we are.

That's why it's common for people in the aftermath of grief to wonder about their identity and even life's purpose.

Over the years, clients have shared how recording a loved one's voice when they are singing, taking pictures, making a family recipe book, taking a holiday—all of which meant a lot to a loved one—are ways of celebrating the bond that is shared, but also comes from a place of fear that there is limited time, that they might as well capture these treasured moments before it's too late. Our acknowledgement of impending grief and our feeling for the loved one can sometimes push us into these acts, which are life-affirming and a celebration of our loved one.

If anticipatory grief feels overwhelming, anxiety-provoking and persistent, it's a good idea to speak to a mental health professional. If the possibility of impending loss is making you feel that you are left with guilt, anger and open wounds, then also it is a good idea to seek support and work gently with a professional, while still holding a space of compassion for your own self. Be kind and non-judgmental to yourself, especially if you find your mind wandering to thoughts of a parent or loved one's loss. When people worry about what would happen to them in the context of another's death, they wonder if they are being selfish. I don't think it is about being selfish. Our lives are intertwined with those we love; losing them to death or otherwise is a reminder of losing a part of us and who we are, and hence the anxiety.

10

Losses We Don't Understand

Priya, a forty-five-year-old woman, in the session shared 'I have worked for ten years in the same company. Last week, I noticed that the security guard, who would greet me daily and have conversations with me, was not there for the full week. I checked with the head of security and he mentioned that the security guard had died of cardiac arrest around twelve days ago, when I was away on work at a client site. Hearing this broke me, and I couldn't believe what I was feeling. I tried explaining the intensity of loss to my colleague and then my husband, and it just felt like no one understood. I knew about his family; his daughter's wedding was lined up in a few months and he always asked about my daughter and husband. It's as if no one understood my pain and even the fact that over the years, we had formed this relationship of trust and warmth. His death felt like grief and yet no one who was close to me understood why I was feeling so much.'

There are losses that society fails to acknowledge, notice or even talk about openly. These are what we refer to as 'disenfranchised loss'. These sometimes take the form of losses that are not legitimized by society. As a result, the support and witnessing that the grieving individuals need doesn't come through, and they often feel unseen and not understood.

Activity

Write down for yourself some losses that you experienced, which didn't have social sanction and were possibly not understood.

____

____

____

____

____

____

____

____

Dr Kenneth Doka, who is an expert when it comes to thanatology (the scientific study of death), coined the term 'disenfranchised grief' in 1989. He defined it as, ' . . . grief that results when a person experiences a significant loss and the resultant grief is not openly acknowledged, socially validated, or publicly mourned. In short, although the individual is experiencing a grief reaction, there is no social recognition that the person has a right to grieve or a claim for social sympathy or support.' This is also known as hidden grief or sorrow.

Dr Doka talks in his work about how these losses aren't just limited to when someone dies and includes losses that we don't very often acknowledge. The pandemic is an example of our disenfranchised losses: whether it was the loss of autonomy, loss of intimacy or missing key milestone events such as the birth of a grandchild or child.

Here are some examples of disenfranchised grief:

- Losing a pet
- LGBTQ+ folks who haven't come out yet and feel that both physically and psychologically there is lack of safety when it comes to their grief

- Grieving for family members whom you never or barely met, whether its grandparents, sibling or even a parent
- Infertility
- Death of patients for doctors, death of clients for psychologists and psychiatrists
- Loss by suicide
- Abortion
- An adoption that doesn't come through
- Death of a friend who you knew intimately but only virtually and had never met, which is common in the age of social media
- Loss of an ex-partner
- Death of teachers for children

Grieving is very hard and can feel deeply isolating particularly when we feel nobody sees us or understands what we have gone through. When there are some losses that aren't seen for what they are and what they mean to the grieving individual, they make the process of grieving and, in turn, grief integration extremely hard.

The hardest bit about disenfranchised grief is that very often, we don't know what to do with it. I remember during the pandemic, I lost a client to death due to health issues. I had worked with the client years ago and a tremendous sense of sorrow washed over me. I didn't know what to do. The client's family knew that he was in therapy and so, they reached out to inform me. Since it was in 2020, when Covid deaths were on the rise, there weren't any prayer meetings or a way to meet the family. Without any mourning ritual to support the loss, it felt so sharp until I spoke about it to my supervisor, who acknowledged how the world feels different now that a client whom I knew and loved working with was no more. He said, 'It's okay if you didn't meet the person for years, the bond remains. Allow yourself to grieve. Find a way to express what you are feeling.'

I finally chose to journal about it for days and give myself the permission to feel the sadness and even acknowledge that my grief was coming in waves. I spoke about it to my family members, without revealing any details, and that allowed for a certain witnessing and for them to understand why I was so overwhelmed and raw on certain days.

Choosing to make space for our own grief is important, even when it doesn't feel seen or heard by others. Choosing to find support via community, support groups, mental health professionals and helplines are some of the ways. I often suggest to clients that they develop their own rituals and engage in soothing practices, such as donating to a cause that their loved one was passionate about, volunteering, planting a tree and journalling. Over the years, clients have shared how getting a tattoo, getting an artwork commissioned, creating art and sometimes also acts such as running or joining a martial arts class have helped them deal with the emotion.

Grief for LGBTQ+

Mohit, my client who is twenty-three, said, 'I lost my partner Sid, whom I was dating, in a car accident. It left me devastated. I'm not yet out to my parents and friends, and I became extremely emotional after this incident. I remember in the first month, my friends and family couldn't understand where the intensity of grief was coming from. I have a sense that they may have known about our relationship, but nobody wanted to acknowledge it. I felt deeply alone and lonely, as I couldn't be honest with anyone about what Sid meant to me. It's been six months, and it looks like I don't have permission to grieve, and I cannot tell everyone that Sid was my world.'

Grieving is hard for everyone, but it gets harder for folks who aren't out to their family, or even in set-ups where, despite them openly talking about their orientation, their families don't accept them and in turn, their significant others. The reality is when it comes to paperwork and logistical work, or even hospitals, my sense from clients and friends is that they often find themselves explaining and overexplaining how they have been living together and been partners for years. The stigma and lack of awareness about LGBTQ+ relationships make the grieving process for the bereaved more complicated, and very often, the support from friends, family and even society is not enough.

In one session, Mohit told me, 'After I slowly started telling folks in the community about us, on Sid's one-year death anniversary, my friends held a memorial service for my partner and called everyone who knew about us. We shared our favourite goofy memories of him, personal pictures, cried together and laughed a lot. I felt that moment was bittersweet. It felt like people saw him and our love, and yet I missed him. It's strange, but grief taught me that I do have my chosen family. People are there for me and it finally feels like hope.'

Losing a Pet

Aakash, an eleven-year-old, told me, 'I have been crying for the last few days since Poppy passed away. She was my best friend and she would wait every day for me to return from school. Mumma wants us to adopt another pet, but I'm scared—what if I lose that one too.'

Almost two decades ago, I saw my first client in therapy, whose parents had reached out to me because their son was grieving the loss of his pet, and so were they. They felt that the child needed to talk to another person as they were not able to say the right things to him that would be helpful. At the same time, he had no one in his school, either teachers or friends, who understood what Poppy meant to him. He told me in therapy that one of his friends told him, 'I don't know why you are crying over a dog, you can get another one.' In the next session, he told me, 'I like you because you asked me my dog's name and you love listening to her funny stories and seeing her pictures.' Aakash looked upon Poppy as his younger sibling and adored her. He would show up to every session, for the first few times, with a picture of Poppy or a toy she played with.

Losing a pet is difficult. Our pets become our families, they are an integral part of our life and so much of our day-to-day routines are built around them. As Mira, who is forty-three, told me, 'Losing Chloe was like losing a child. She was delicate, friendly and always following me around the house. She was my baby and I now feel this pit in my stomach and this void in my life that nothing can fill. She was my world and now I'm lonely, left all by myself.'

The grief that pet parents feel is immense and it consumes them. Yet, losing a pet falls under the category of disenfranchised grief as it's a loss that is not completely understood by society. Very often, the intensity of this loss is underestimated by others, and it's also trivialized. When adults are grieving the loss of their pet, they feel that their friends don't recognize that losing a pet feels the same as losing a human being whom you loved. Our pets give us unconditional love and we form a bond with them; it's a relationship we share and when they are no more, whether due to an accident, illness or old age, it hurts and breaks you from within.

The trouble, though, is that when grief is not fully recognized and acknowledged by society, there is a risk of it turning into complicated grief. I have heard clients tell me how they struggle to ask for leave and take time off, because colleagues at work or bosses often underplay or fail to recognize the impact that losing a pet can have on one's personal well-being.

Our love for the pets who choose us is profound and deep—no wonder then that the grief we feel for them is all-consuming. Over the years, books and movies have mindfully tried to build a narrative that is sensitive and recognize the impact that losing our animal companion can have not just on children, but also adults.

If you have lost a pet or know someone who has lost their pet, here are some ways to cope:

Figure out where you find your own soothing space: This is a huge task of grieving. Whether it's spending time in pet cafes or with friends who understand your grief, and where you feel seen. I have had clients who, in the aftermath of loss, got a tattoo done or a painting of their favourite pet commissioned to celebrate the joy their pet brought to them, but also as a way of saying that this is the way their pet continues to live on.

Reach out to other pet parents: Very often, pet parents feel that people who don't have pets or have never had them don't seem to understand or comprehend their loss. Choose to reach out to other friends, support groups and forums available online, which allow you to share about your loss and at the same time, offer resources and insights about what helped others.

A memorial or gathering marking the loss of your pet: What I generally suggest to clients is to call their friends, family and even colleagues who knew of their pet, and use the gathering to share stories, anecdotes and moments; a reminder of how the pet touched your life and theirs. Whether it's a memorial for the pet or an evening of all your social support coming together, it allows pet owners to feel supported and at the same time, experience how their pet was part of many people's lives and brought joy to many others. This sense of coming together can really help in processing grief and building a safe space in which pet parents feel held and understood, and their grief is recognized. This is so important, given that often it ends up taking the form of disenfranchised grief.

Reaching out to a mental health professional: I remember a sixty-seven-year-old man, Joseph, who reached out to me after he lost his dog due to an accident. One of his first words were, 'Nobody knows that I have come for counselling. I don't think my family understands what Rudolf meant to me, it was as if he got me. When my wife passed away, he sat with me quietly and supported me through the grief. Now, when I have lost him to an unfortunate accident, I feel bereft and alone. My mind is filled with what-ifs, guilt and dreams, where he comes back into my life. I haven't slept well for two weeks; I end up sleeping for two or three hours every night. One of my friends just sent me your number and said that it helped him when he was struggling with grief. I don't know why I'm here, but I also don't know what is there to look forward to in my life without Rudolf.'

Choosing to speak to a therapist during grief may help, particularly if there is lack of social support, traumatic circumstances under which death happened, guilt and profound grief that seems to consume you.

What not to say: What hurts the most for pet parents is when others trivialize the loss they have experienced. Using certain statements, such as 'just a dog' or 'just a cat', can be infuriating for the person who has lost a pet. It can make them feel that you are undermining and taking away from the beautiful relationship they shared with their beloved pet. What most pet parents also find hurtful is when others try and force them to adopt or get another pet, soon after the loss. This advice, if perceived as being premature, can make the pet owner feel that you are implying that their pet is replaceable and hence, this is hurtful. Choose to be gentle, ask questions, listen to the pet parent's pain and be present for them by offering an attentive presence and supporting them gently, by acknowledging their loss.

I have had pet parents often share with me how they keep the collar of a beloved pet whom they lost to death. Often, these mementoes are soothing and a reminder of their continuing love. As a pet parents, figure out what you want to continue keeping as a reminder that allows you to still celebrate the joy and companionship your pet brought in your life.

11

Vicarious Grief

Samara, a fifteen-year-old girl, told me during a virtual therapy session, 'My friend told me about a friend of our age, who died by suicide two days ago. I had heard about her as my friend was close to her, but never met her. I haven't been able to stop crying since then. My parents have been extremely worried and wonder if I'm depressed or suicidal. I feel so sad for her and her parents. I can't stop thinking about how alone and sad she must have been to want to end her own life. Do you think I'm crazy for crying over someone I never really met and had just heard of?'

What makes us human is our empathy and capacity to feel and be there for others. As a result, we are not just impacted by losses that happen to us but also by the losses of others, not just our acquaintances but also celebrities or losses that humankind goes through. Our tears that flow during a movie or when we read a novel reflect how our capacity to feel deeply for others shows up, even when we watch or read something that is imaginary.

Vicarious grief is what we experience when we witness or hear of losses that others have gone through, either due to death or a loss of another kind. As I mention in my column on grief written for *Mint Lounge,* 'Our vicarious grief is a reminder of shared humanity and our deep capacity for compassion towards others. We are all social beings and in moments of sorrow and loss, we realize our stories and life are so deeply interconnected—hence the pain.'[1]

We all have experienced vicarious grief in some way or another. The pandemic was a time when everyone experienced vicarious loss, and the impact of it has continued to linger.

Certain professionals, such as doctors, mental health professionals, hospital staff and journalists, are more likely to be in situations where they not just witness, but also see and hear of losses, which continue to impact them even if they didn't know or meet the person. There are also times where our vicarious grief takes the form of collective grief. Think about the Covid-19 pandemic, a train tragedy, the lives that were lost when the *Titanic* sank and the deaths in the Russia-Ukraine war. In moments of natural and man-made disasters, health crises and epidemics, our sense of vicarious grief heightens. All these deaths and events evoke a sense of collective grief in people across the world. While how people grieve is unique and different, there are certain times where an entire community, world, nation or cities mourn the loss of a person or group of people. The loss in these moments is felt as tragic and sharp; the feeling cuts through us collectively, evoking a grief reaction. After the 26/11 attacks in 2008, many clients showed up in therapy describing how they couldn't stop crying watching the scenes on TV; some couldn't sleep and some just couldn't stop thinking about those people whose lives had been lost.

Even when events happen in a different city or country, they can be felt as a vicarious, collective grief that in turn can have a huge impact on how we live and our choices, evoking our own fears and anxieties. 'Vicarious grief' as a term is attributed to thanatology expert and psychologist Robert Kastenbaum (1987), who in a paper titled, 'Vicarious Grief: An Intergenerational Phenomenon?',[2] talks about how he unexpectedly found some elderly women particularly express sorrow for the loss of others, who were not personally known to them.

Building Space for Witnessing and Dealing with Vicarious Grief

Vicarious grief and collective grief both require witnessing and an awareness that they need to be processed. We cannot wish it away or hope that with passing time, we will forget about it or can suppress it. All grief that we choose to not acknowledge, articulate or even let ourselves feel finds a way to leak and show up eventually, either in our thoughts, feelings, actions or in terms of psychosomatic symptoms.

Dealing with vicarious grief requires acknowledging what's happening to us as we witness it. It requires paying attention to emotions evoked in us, and sometimes even accepting that some of the emotions that may emerge can feel scary and confusing. As Samara and I continued doing our work in therapy sessions, she told me in her third session, 'I haven't told this to anyone, but for the last week, I have been having this thought over and over. I keep thinking, what if my mother or father die by suicide? As soon as I have this thought, I try and push it away and feel extremely guilty for thinking this way. As a therapist, have you worked with people who have had suicidal thoughts and managed to get better, and not take their life? Can clinical depression and suicidal thoughts be treated?'

Hearing about the loss of a peer had triggered her own fears and questions about mental health and even her parents' mortality. Over the sessions, I worked with her to answer some of her concerns and teach her techniques for self-soothing. We also did some work jointly with the family, so that they could learn to support her in a way that was sensitive and answer her questions, rather than tell her to stop thinking.

Samara also chose to journal about her feelings and learnt not to judge herself every time a feeling of grief came over, when she thought about the girl who had died by suicide. During one of the sessions, she told me, 'I wish that girl had met a therapist, who she could talk to. When I grow up, I want to listen and be there for others, I don't want people to feel that they are not loved, or no one is there for them.' In that moment, I realized that sometimes even when it is vicarious grief, our meaning-making can help us make sense of things and also, in a way, help us deal with our loss.

As I mention in a column, 'Just as we have the capacity to be happy for strangers, witnessing their pain and loss can also impact us. Community support can go a long way in helping us deal with vicarious grief. At the same time, learning to be on our own side and be compassionate as we take time to heal and deal with the pain is crucial.'[3]

12

Celebrity Deaths

Why do we mourn the death of celebrities, and why does it hurt so much?

When a celebrity has passed away, have you found yourself grieving and yet wondered what evoked such a strong emotion of loss for you?

This is a question I'm asked very often by clients in therapy and by journalists. While it's hard to say if everyone is impacted by them, it is true that many of us are affected thus. This becomes attenuated if the death is untimely and due to unfortunate circumstances or accidents.

Clients often talk about celebrity deaths in therapy sessions. My sense is that these deaths remind us of our own mortality and how time is so limited. More so, when the deaths are untimely, the idea of uncertainty and unpredictability of life also emerges. It's also very common for clients, who struggle with clinical depression and suicidal thoughts, to experience an increased intensity when it comes to their own moods, particularly when there is a celebrity death either because of suicide, under strange circumstances or untimely. They often mention how they feel more depressed and anxious in the light of celebrity deaths. The mention of increased anxiety and panic attacks also goes up in days following celebrity deaths and some clients talk about the fact that they feel an impulse emerging, a desire to end their life, too. This is deeply connected to the fact that we put artistes, popular figures, athletes and actors on a pedestal, and believe that they have everything—maybe even a perfect life.

As Suveer, who is twenty-eight, told me, 'Every time a celebrity dies by suicide, I begin to see life as being fragile. I start wondering if people, who seemingly have everything, can take a step like this and feel despair, what happens to people like us, who are struggling when it comes to finances, jobs and even basic needs sometimes? I worry for myself; speculation and news updates make me more pessimistic and helpless. I have learnt to stay off social media and news as I don't think I can handle the overwhelming sadness that ensues after these deaths.'

Our memories are deeply intertwined with an artiste's work and very often, their oeuvre has served as a source of motivation and inspiration for us. I remember the morning when news of Robin Williams' death by suicide broke, I felt shocked and couldn't stop crying. He was my favourite actor and I associated some of my fondest memories with his movies. I remember texting a friend that day to ask if she had read the news and double check if it was true. I was in disbelief. It just didn't seem possible that someone who played such beautiful and hopeful roles in *Patch Adams* and then *Good Will Hunting* could end his own life. All my experience of working as a therapist didn't help at that moment; I felt a sharp pain, sorrow and grief.

My career had been deeply influenced by his work and his movie, *Good Will Hunting*. I was twenty when I first saw the movie and almost twenty years later, I still remember how powerful and inspiring it was for me. I was training to be a therapist at the time, and watching that movie felt like I was coming close to a goal. I almost had a role model in the character Robin Williams played. I remember thinking about him as the perfect psychotherapist and wanted to emulate him. In fact, my first job was on a university campus with college students, and at the same time I worked as a counsellor for children of sex workers, who struggled with concerns around attachment safety. When Williams died, I remember thinking of Freud's theory and how I had developed such a fondness and attachment to not just the roles he played, but also to him. I had cultivated an idea of him in my head based on his movies, and while the news of his death was hard enough, the fact that it was through suicide made it harder. Without realizing it, I had been idolizing him over the years, and I spent all day crying at intervals and reminding myself that it was okay to grieve for an actor, whose work had not just impacted me but also given me hope in my darkest hours. I also silently grieved for the sadness and loneliness he might have felt in those last moments and thought about how much he would have suffered to take this step.

When deaths have happened in a freak accident or some other untimely manner, it brings to fore the question of fairness and unpredictability, which can often be anxiety-provoking. As humans, we like to believe that we have control. Hearing such news can often evoke deep fears and existential questions around the purpose of life, legacy and even a recognition of how our idea of control can be illusory.

Here are some techniques and strategies that can help you, if you find yourself struggling with grief after a celebrity passes away:

1. **Mindfully attend to your own grief:** If you have felt grief when a celebrity has passed away, it's very normal. Allow yourself to mourn and grieve.

   Let no one tell you that you shouldn't be doing that or feeling enormous sadness. Even if you haven't met them in person, because of the time we spend watching an artiste's work, following their life on social media and finally, the impact they have on us and the inspiration, pleasure and entertainment they provide us, their loss hits us hard.

2. **Engage with their work:** As we deal with the loss and make sense of it, one could revisit their work. I often think of it as a way of celebrating their legacy and marking the moment, and acknowledging how they influenced my life. I remember when the singer K.K. suddenly passed away due to a cardiac arrest, I spent the next few days listening to his music, which was a reminder of my college days, of evenings where I wondered about what life had to offer and sometimes a way for me to hold on to hope. At the same time, some people feel they can't bear to watch an artiste's work. If you feel that, too, it's alright. Take time to sit with the grief and don't force yourself to see or hear an artiste's work till you feel emotionally ready.
3. **Limit the consumption of news and stay away from social media:** Often, the news around celebrity deaths can lead to a harrowing sadness, but also fear and helplessness for some of those struggling with mental health conditions. In fact, as a rule, I often address it in therapy sessions to gauge how the client is impacted by the development. My advice is to choose to consume news in small doses. Avoid looking at videos or messages late into the night as clients often report experiencing dark thoughts and sleeplessness in the aftermath of these deaths. Sometimes, people can find themselves getting lost in conspiracy theories if the deaths are under mysterious circumstances; this can become obsessive and anxiety-provoking. I tell clients to become mindful and learn to have guardrails when it comes to videos of the deceased.

4. **Find time to journal and articulate what you are feeling:** It's common for people to talk about how they feel deeply emotional in such moments, and yet they can't comprehend what is leading to such strong emotional responses. Writing or journalling can help in these moments as it allows us to give words to our feelings. Allow yourself to write uninterrupted, in a free-flowing manner, so that your thoughts and feelings can find their way out.
5. **Community support:** It's okay to call and reach out for support when you find yourself shocked or gutted by the death of your favourite celebrity. I remember a client mentioning how when one actor died rather suddenly, he organized an evening of stories, where everyone who knew the artiste could come and share stories and celebrate the impact his life had on each of them. Seeking community support can help us feel less alone and allow us to find shared rituals that help honour the work of people who inspired us.

Many people find themselves grieving over the loss of youth and potential when a young actor or athlete passes away. The way the media reports it and sensationalizes it also adds to the grief and shock. I hope that over the years, we can learn to talk about celebrity deaths in a humane and sensitive way, with dignity.

13

Traumatic Grief

When the death of a loved one happens in ways that are sudden or violent, or under traumatic circumstances that are hard to understand or fathom, our emotions can take the form of traumatic grief. Of course, needless to add, all losses do feel traumatic, irrespective of how they happened.

Some of the examples of traumatic grief are as follows:

- Losing a loved one to suicide
- A gruesome accident
- Death due to natural disasters
- Death of a person who was extremely healthy
- Homicides
- Medical negligence
- Death due to violence
- Unexplained circumstances surrounding the death
- Overdoses of alcohol and drugs

In all these instances, there is the grief of losing a loved one and along with it, the trauma about the circumstances under which the death happened, and the pain their loved one went through. Gokul, who is twenty-two, lost his sister in a burglary gone wrong. He told me, 'Losing her was hard, but what's harder is that I don't know how much she suffered before they killed her. I wonder if she tried to fight them. I keep thinking that if I had reached home on time, maybe this could have been averted. I'm left with questions to which there is no answer now. I don't know how much she suffered before she died. I'm left with survivor's guilt.'

Gokul talked about how after his sister's death, even the slightest loud sound would scare him. He also avoided staying out and he would continually have flashbacks, because he was the one who found his sister. He would have panic attacks and didn't know what to do with his life. The rumination and incessant replaying tired him out, and he also began to have suicidal thoughts. He couldn't sleep and his anxiety would massively increase in the nights. Given how his health was deteriorating, it seemed that his grief was accompanied by trauma, and it was quite clear that there were symptoms that needed medical attention. So, the treatment plan involved working with a psychiatrist, using psychiatric medication, therapy and then psychosocial support at different levels, both at home and from work, to help him work through his grief.

Kusum, a thirty-five-year-old who lost her father to suicide, told me, 'I keep thinking about how much pain he must have been in. What would he have been thinking when he took his life? How is it that none of us saw his pain and depression? It's hard to believe that he's gone. Seeing him lie there helplessly, checking if he's alive and then wondering that if we had reached home a few minutes earlier, we would maybe have saved him, all of it makes things worse. I just can't make sense of the loss.'

Kusum reached out four weeks into the loss and said that she felt her life spinning out of control. She was beginning to lose all interest in her work; she felt hopeless and helpless. Kusum had read enough and wanted to work through the trauma, so that she didn't slip into depression. She had enough social support and that helped her work through what she was experiencing. She said that she was sleeping alright, eating well and could maintain a structure to her day.

What's important to remember is that traumatic grief can show up differently for different individuals. One needs to be mindful and not pathologize the grieving process too early. My experience has been that when there is traumatic grief, very often it's the entire family that needs counselling. The process can help them address guilt, survivor's guilt in the possibility that they escaped the traumatic incident and then counselling around a morbid fear of death that family members may struggle with.

Learning to work gently and keeping an eye for cues that may need clinical attention is crucial. If there are panic attacks, inability to sleep for days, poor or no appetite, suicidal ideation, self-harm, incessant, intrusive thoughts for a long duration and repetitive flashbacks about the event in a day over a period of time, then it's a good idea to work with a psychiatrist to understand how this can be managed.

There is also the 'bereavement overload', a term coined by Robert Kastenbaum, a psychologist and gerontologist. This primarily refers to circumstances or situations under which the individual loses multiple people at the same time, or in quick succession, to death. This is also referred to as cumulative grief.[1] The reality is that before the individual can process or even come to terms with the loss, other deaths follow. Sadly, with the pandemic, there are many families who are struggling with this phenomenon. In the present-case scenario, family members who survive are very often left with a feeling of survivor's guilt. These are also situations that can take the form of traumatic grief.

Learning to recognize traumatic grief very often helps clients understand and articulate the intensity of what they are feeling and how grief is showing up for them. This, in turn, helps with how they can address and deal with the grief.

14

Delayed Emotional Responses to Loss

Moiz, who is forty-six and has been in therapy for over two years, told me, 'I lost my mum when I was eight years old. She was hit by a truck and that's what I was told. No one asked me anything about how I felt. I took three days off from school and my teachers were not informed. I didn't know if I should tell my classmates. My father suddenly became this quiet man, who barely spoke after my mother's death. I have never spoken to anyone in detail about this and how it made me feel, I just moved on with my life and I thought that's how everyone copes. But ever since we started working in therapy, I have been wondering if I processed my grief.'

Grief never leaves us; it stays with us. But there is also delayed grief, where the grief and emotions accompanying it and their intensity are not processed. To the extent that many times, I have worked with clients who talk about a significant loss in their life as a life event, but at the same time they are not even aware that they haven't processed or worked through the grief. In my practice, I have had clients who, decades after the loss happened, have talked about an event that they accepted at an intellectual level, but never got to process at an emotional level. The truth is that when grief begins to emerge after years of having been parked, stored and suppressed, it's painful, scary and can feel like sorrow, like the melancholy that one experiences in the first few days of loss. It's overwhelming and heavy. For the client to decide to do the work and process it takes a lot of emotional courage, and a certain readiness.

How Delayed Grief Shows Up

Delayed grief lingers as unacknowledged grief. Very often, representations of delayed grief show up in relation to adults, who for years have been carrying it within. What seems to be a common thread for many of these clients is that they experienced a loss of their loved one when they were a child. As Moiz mentioned, most of them talk about how a culture of silence followed the loss and hence, they didn't know how to feel or deal with it. We do know that for children, how they process and even give themselves the permission to grieve is determined by the role the primary caregivers, their family, plays during that time. Given that very often, children are too young to understand what death means and make sense of their loss, they need handholding from adults to navigate it. How children and teenagers process their loss also depends on the social support available to them. I have worked with clients, who said that since their parent was in acute grief, as a fourteen- or fifteen-year-old, they chose to take care of their parent and not pay attention to their own grief.

Sometimes, the way life happens and the circumstances that surround grief may not give grieving individuals a chance to process their emotions. Mina, who is forty, shared, 'My mother was shattered and she stopped talking after my father's sudden death in a train crash. I didn't even pay attention to my grief or think there was any time for it, as I had to take care of her, manage my job and was about to give birth to a baby. I reduced myself to a caregiver and being hyper-focused. But all I felt was exhaustion and numbness. My capacity to feel positive emotions disappeared. I just didn't give myself permission to grieve and bottled it up for months, until a year later when I started having outbursts of crying and couldn't sleep at all.'

When death has happened due to suicide, drug or alcohol overdose and there is disenfranchised grief, people may not be able to talk about it openly to others and as a result, they have delayed grief. There is shame, guilt and mixed feelings attached to the loss, which we discuss in Part 4, that can all come in the way of grief.

What tends to happen with delayed grief is that there is an intellectualization of the loss. Delayed grief or grief that was not processed often shows up as fear, anxiety or panic attacks. In subtle ways, it can control an individual's life, not allowing them to reach their full potential. I have worked with individuals, who explain how they felt numb when grief happened. However, in the years that followed, they developed a morbid fear of death, obsessive thoughts and fears of dying and then unexplained melancholy a few years down the line, for which they actually sought treatment—and realized it was grief.

Moiz felt that if he fell in love with someone, he would lose them, too, so he didn't allow himself to fall in love or believe in it. Ever since he was eight, he continued having nightmares and night terrors, which were never treated. He also felt guilty, both as a child and then as an adult, if he ever expressed his own needs. As a result, he withdrew and led a lonely life without any friends. He had reached out in therapy because for years, he had felt consumed by a sadness that never left him and preoccupied him at multiple levels.

The reality is that when we suppress unpleasant sensations or emotions, our capacity to experience pleasant or positive emotions is also impacted. This has shown up in clients reporting how they feel numb, unable to enjoy pleasant emotions and savour anything. They talk about how they feel like they are just going through the motions of life, find it hard to engage and miss the feeling of vitality.

If you recognize there is delayed grief that's coming in the way of you leading a full life, I suggest that you speak to a mental health professional and address it.

15

When Do You Require Clinical Attention?

As discussed in Part 1, grieving individuals do reach out for therapy in the aftermath of loss because it's overwhelming and there is devastating sadness that one struggles to cope with. They often reach out in therapy, because they feel not understood; at other times, they want to understand the grief process better. Some clients feel that they are scared and consumed by the feelings that are emerging in them.

Therapy becomes a space to deal with ambivalent feelings and find meaning-making. Clients also use sessions to explore how they can continue to keep the bond going on with their loved one, who is no more, and at the same time reimagine and rebuild their life.

My work over the years has taught me that how people deal with grief and the time they take to make sense and deal with conflicting feelings is subjective. As discussed earlier, how we cope is a function of a variety of factors.

We don't need to pathologize grief—it's an inevitable part of life and people's journeys are very specific. We can't put a timeline to grief. There is no way one can predetermine the timeline when it comes to grief acceptance and grief integration. There aren't any linear steps that one can take to reach the stage of integration. No matter how the death happened, our desire for a timeline when it comes to healing comes from a space of wanting a semblance of certainty. Loss reminds us how uncertain life is and our wish for a timeline comes from a space of finding hope.

In my clinical experience, for a lot of clients, the journey towards grief integration and meaning begins many years after the incident.

The pandemic has been a reminder of that. Mukund, a thirty-three-old client, told me, 'My dad died in the hospital as he had Covid and I was at home getting treated for the same. I never got a chance to see him, didn't get to perform his last rites or say my goodbye, hold a prayer meeting or even receive support. I developed complications a week after his death and was hospitalized then. My recovery took six months and I feel my grief never got processed because the logistics, ill health and coping with work pressure consumed me.'

Our understanding of grief and how people work towards integration needs to be holistic, keeping in mind the unique psychosocial factors that surrounded the grief.

With clients who have a past mental health condition and are on psychiatric medication, I choose to work closely to mindfully monitor and observe what's emerging. For people who have depressive traits or have struggled with depression, the death of a loved one can lead to the possibility of another depressive episode. At the same time, my experience has been that this may not be true for everyone who has the traits or history of mental health conditions. While the devastating sadness that follows grief looks like depression, it's important to not confuse the two. While grief and depression do share some similar characteristics, they are not the same. We need to remember that every grieving individual is not depressed. When you are supporting someone who is grieving, learning to be patient and not pathologizing what they are feeling is crucial. When grief is followed by intrusive thoughts of self-harm, suicidal ideation or attempts, severe panic attacks, excessive alcohol use, drugs, inability to eat, insomnia and sleeping for days, it's important to work closely with the client, psychiatrist and the family to figure out what aspects may benefit from medical attention.

We change and so does our life in the aftermath of grief. When grief strikes us, all that we know of life comes to an end, so the intensity of feelings and sorrow is understandable. That's why we need to be mindful when it comes to medicalizing or pathologizing grief. At the same time, we must keep our eyes and ears open, when there are persistent and intrusive symptoms that do need attention.

Part 3

Making Sense of the World

16

The Culture of Silence

The Silence that Surrounds Grief

Komal, a thirty-three-year-old female client, who lost both her parents in a span of six months, told me, 'I met my boss for the first time in person after my parents' loss. He never checked about my well-being or the loss. He had sent me a message to express condolences when we were working online, but in person, he didn't bring it up. It disappointed me and made me feel small, in a way. I felt that my grief was invisible. Also, with friends, I feel like they don't know what to say or do around me, and it makes me feel very uncomfortable. I wonder if my grief has changed me or their perception of me.'

Ravi, a fifty-one-year-old male client, whose wife died of cancer, said, 'The other day, when I entered the office canteen, all my teammates who were laughing and having fun suddenly paused and became silent. I don't know if they are uncomfortable being happy around me because of what happened, or they feel pity for me. But I have reached a place where I want to leave this organization as I'm tired of these silences. It's strange when you know people can see how much pain you are in and yet choose to be quiet and awkward around you. I don't know if I'm expecting too much or it's just that people don't know what to do with an adult grown man, who's grieving.'

Often, we don't know how to respond or communicate with those who are grieving the loss of a loved one to death, dealing with a difficult chronic health diagnosis or going through divorce or estrangement. An equal number of men and women in therapy talk about how the silence that they experience in the presence of colleagues and friends is both exhausting and shocking for them.

Here are some possible reasons that explains the silences:

1. **Othering:** Katherine May in her book, *Wintering: The Power of Rest and Retreat in Difficult Times*, says, 'Wintering is a season in the cold. It is a fallow period in life, when you are cut off from the world, feeling rejected, sidelined, blocked from progress, or cast into the role as an outsider. Perhaps it results from an illness; perhaps from a life event such as bereavement or the birth of a child; perhaps it comes from humiliation or failure.'[1] I love this description and sometimes wonder if with the grief, there is this 'othering' that takes place, where the person who has experienced a loss feels like an outsider. The lens with which grief is viewed in our society also contributes to this othering.
2. **Lack of vocabulary around grief:** I have often wondered whether, explicitly or implicitly, we are kept away from the idea of mortality. We are neither trained nor taught to have a vocabulary for grief. Just as we don't openly talk about the feeling of grief, I wonder if we—as a society and community—maybe haven't learnt how to express our condolences or even offer help. When someone is grieving, no matter what the reason is, people want to come across as considerate. At the same time, they don't want to cross any boundaries. Sometimes, a part of me wonders if people's silence comes from either

not knowing what to say or the fear that they may cross a boundary and say something that is perceived wrongly.

At the same time, these silences bring a drift in relationships and can also leave the grieving person feel like they are not cared for. A sixty-two-year-old female client told me, 'When my husband passed away, a close friend of mine didn't come to offer condolences for a year, although she lived in the same city. It's been five years since, but somehow, I can't make sense of it. She visited me after a year, but I couldn't connect with her. She never explained her reasons and I felt exploited and cheated, because I had been present for all her difficult times over the years.'

Some of these silences show up in strange ways and their impact takes the form of secondary loss, which we discuss later in the book.

3. **Irrational beliefs around grief:** Grief often takes the form of that 'who-must-not-be-named', a term used in the Harry Potter series by J.K. Rowling to describe Lord Voldemort, a powerful wizard and the arch-nemesis of the protagonist.

   Take, for instance, one of those irrational beliefs, which very often show up in the case of anticipatory grief, as a client mentioned: 'My mum believes that we don't need to talk about death. She believes that we will bring something negative or untoward upon us by mentioning it.'

   Maybe, in some strange way, we believe that if we don't acknowledge or talk about it, we don't need to accept that death is inevitable and that each one of us will have to deal with it, sooner or later. The silence around it is our denial and a way of having control over a situation that's beyond us.

Activity

What are some of the beliefs that exist in your family around grief and mortality?

There are two ways you can do this. One is to examine and think about the beliefs that may be impacting your decision to remain silent and not talk about grief.

The other is to have a dialogue with close family members and figure out if there is an intergenerational family belief that either directly or indirectly gets passed down in your immediate family. This conversation can open narratives/beliefs that explain the silence around grief. When you have a dialogue with family members, choose to not blame and shame, or hold them accountable for beliefs. As adults, we all have a choice to let go and filter through ideas and beliefs that don't sit well with us. At the same time, even though you have held these beliefs, learn to be kind to yourself and don't start berating yourself or being unfairly critical.

4. **Explore what grief and conversations around mortality evoke in you:** Such conversations are often emotional. I have felt that asking someone about their loss also means building space within oneself to hold their experience. Listening to other people's losses means developing capacity to hold space for others' overwhelming feelings of sadness, anger and even pain.

   When someone is grieving, if you find these conversations uncomfortable, it may be a good moment to ask yourself: 'What do these emotion laden conversations evoke in me?' Particularly at the workplace, it's important for more and more leaders to acknowledge that when they are unable to create safe spaces for these conversations, what is it that they are running from? Coming to terms with one's own emotional landscape or awkwardness may open answers for organizations and individuals.

   If as a close friend or an intimate partner, you find yourself struggling to be present and host a psychologically safe space for these conversations, then address your personal fears, beliefs and assumptions. My experience tells me that grief sometimes can allow people to get close, but also comes in the way of relationships, particularly when a partner feels unsupported and unheard in their moments of loss.

As a therapist, I have often wondered if seeing other people's grief reminds us about our own mortality and the possibility of losses one must deal with. Ask yourself, does this hold true for you?

Activity

Take time to sit and explore the feelings that are triggered in you when you hear about someone else's grief.

____

____

____

____

____

____

____

____

17

Can I Know Exactly What Loss Will Feel Like?

This is one question I'm most often asked in therapy. Even after two decades of work, I'm not sure if there is a simple answer to this. The answer for me has been shaped by my own experience of grief and what I have seen of clients processing and working through their own grief or the anticipation of it.

I remember Fatima, a seventy-two-year-old female client of mine, asking me in her first therapy session, 'I know my husband is dying. I'm prepared for the reality, but I don't think I'm ready for the pain and the grief that I will feel. Could we work through this, so that the pain is not so much, and it hurts a little less?'

I remember I had tears in my eyes then as I replied, 'I wish I could help you with that, but I'm afraid I don't know what the grief will evoke for you and the emotions that it will unfold. However, we can work together to understand more about what this anticipatory grief is evoking now, and the fears that you are experiencing.'

We did just that, and in the process, we figured out how preparation sometimes takes a different meaning than what one commonly understands.

After years of work and even when I have known the client for years, I can never predict what grief would look like for each one. The reality is that even clients can't predict what it looks like, and no matter how much we force ourselves to think pre-emptively, we discover what it feels and looks like only when we experience it.

When the loss happens, what we feel emotionally or the course that grief will take is very unpredictable. We can never be fully prepared. Not knowing what it will do to us may sometimes feel scarier than the grief itself.

There is no manual or artificial intelligence repository that can determine what grief will look like for you.

My lens around the definition of preparation significantly changed when I began working with individuals who were dealing with chronic progressive illnesses and limited treatment options. As I worked with them and their families, I realized that how people define preparation is very personal. However, there are some areas around grief that we can work with, which might be very useful. We can look at preparation through five different lenses.

1. **Preparing for what grief will evoke and unfold for you:** You need to learn to surrender to the idea that you will never know what grief will look like till the time you experience the loss of a loved one.
   While we do have a sense of what we may experience, we can neither predict the full range of emotions that will come with it nor the intensity of what we might feel. Also, there is no way to predict how long people will take to integrate their grief.
   As Kevin Pearson in the popular sitcom show, *This is Us* (2016), says, 'Grief is a tricky thing, you know?

You just can't prepare for how it's gonna make you feel or how you'll handle it. Sometimes, you just gotta grab on to whatever's around you just to survive.'

Accepting this reality is all really that you can prepare for.

2. **Preparing for logistics:** This is a big one and very often, people who are dying bring it up in sessions, in the context of a will, jewellery that they need to distribute amongst children and grandchildren, discussion about their estate, how they want their prayer meeting to be, or the funeral/burial process. Very often, family members feel that if some of these matters are spoken about, there is a greater sense of ease and less ambiguity. In the absence of clarity, with sudden grief or in families where these concerns are not addressed, despite illness or age, the bereaved family members are left with the complicated task of unpacking and figuring out a lot of tasks. This can include finances, banking work and property matters, which can be frustrating and tiring for grieving individuals.

   A thirty-five-year-old female client once told me, 'I wish I would have asked my mum how she wanted the funeral to be, or where her locker and cupboard keys were. When my mum passed away, we were all devastated, and no one knew what she would have liked. I know it sounds stupid to mention keys, but I can't tell you the degree of paperwork and searching in the house that had to be done for the simplest of things. There was unending grief and then logistical and administrative tasks that didn't allow me to grieve. On most days, I was angry, confused and stuck with paperwork, feeling lost. The person I would generally complain about this to the most, my mum, was no longer there to hear me or help me. It took four years to sort through everything. I wish someone had told me about these things.'

3. **Learning about the process of grief:** In many instances, both the dying individual and their family members have told me during family therapy that sometimes, understanding how grief works and what the journey can look like helps them feel stronger and trust that while it may take a long time, they will deal with it. So, whether it's through therapy or spiritual practices, the process of understanding the cycle of life and death can help people feel more anchored.
4. **Reimagine how you want to spend time mindfully:** I remember Vishwa, a forty-year-old male client, who had just moved back home to take care of his ninety-year-old grandmom, told me, 'This was the best decision I ever made. I knew my grandmom had only a few years to live anyway and when her cancer diagnosis came through. I felt that I needed to celebrate her life and spend as much time with her as possible. That was the only way I could make sense of her grief. When she passed away, I felt at peace, because I was there in the moments she needed me and gave her all the time I could.'

   Our grief gets a little easier if we feel that we did all that we could by being there for our loved ones, providing them solace and support when they needed it the most.
5. **Begin leaning on social support and allowing yourself to be vulnerable:** When a loved one is dealing with a chronic health condition that's deteriorating, or we know that a dear one may not live very long due to age-related concerns, I suggest to clients to reach out

to their friends, family and people they trust to talk about what they are feeling and the help they may need in the advent of a death. A seventy-two-year-old man told me, 'My father is 102 years old. In the last month, he has started forgetting things and I'm feeling scared that I may lose him, and he will be no more. I feel fear and it's not easy to talk about it to friends and yet, I have started speaking about my fears and possible loneliness to a close friend and while it's comforting to share, it's hard.'

Acknowledging one's vulnerability, and finding people who can be there for us in ways we want is crucial as we allow ourselves to process our own grief.

We aren't ever prepared for grief. Yet, being aware of these pointers can help us in beginning to acknowledge that when loss happens, we will deal with it.

18

No One Grieves the Same Way

'Each person's grief is as unique as their fingerprint. But what everyone has in common is that no matter how they grieve, they share a need for their grief to be witnessed.'[1]

One of the biggest challenges with trying to write this book was the realization that everybody's journey of grief is private and unique. How grief is expressed and the way it shows up and is felt depends on various factors, such as the relationship with the deceased, one's own coping style, temperament, the social support available and so on.

What has stood out for me in my work is that the way grief is expressed also differs as people begin to make sense of it. The ideas of acceptance and grief integration may look different for different people. Our ideas of grief, grieving and even how we reach out in the context of supporting others are influenced by many factors. The behaviours we have seen others in our family exhibit when there has been a loss; the implicit or explicit beliefs and ideas that are passed down from one generation to other, the openness that families allow for when it comes to expression of feelings and bringing one's authentic self into these set-ups—all of these play a part. The pace at which emotions are expressed and show up can look different for different grieving individuals.

Do All Genders Grieve the Same Way?

Working with clients over the years, I have realized that drawing gender-based distinctions when it comes to grief isn't the best idea. It's a process that can lead to biases and we may fall into the trap of confirmation bias. We need to see people's grieving styles for what they are. We need to be aware of our own biases and judgments. Otherwise, we run the risk of not supporting them just because we are not witnessing their grief and in turn, their coping.

Some people during grief find themselves in a state where they feel despair and emotionally devastated, while there are others who approach it as a difficult situation, for which they need to find solutions; then there are some who intellectualize and approach it from a cerebral perspective. Others may use a blended approach, combining these. All of them work, and we need to see them as they are without imposing our lens of judgement.

As a therapist, I have always found merit in observing, being present and listening to gauge where the person is working from and what their preferred style is, before I can choose to support them in sync with their grieving style. While I was researching for this book, I chanced upon Doka and Martin's pioneering work around grieving styles, which reaffirmed my experiences in therapy with clients.

Kenneth Doka and Terry Martin in their book, *Grieving Beyond Gender: Understanding the Way Men and Women Mourn*, talk about different styles of grieving. They, in fact, began their research with the lens of trying to understand grief and gender. However, as they worked around this more and more, they began to see that while gender was one of the factors that influenced grieving style, using it as a primary lens was limiting and didn't do justice to the process of grieving, which is very individualized.

They talked about two primary styles of grieving—instrumental and intuitive. The instrumental grieving style shows up in in the context of people talking about their thoughts around grief, rather than what they feel. Doka and Martin describe how instrumental grievers talk about it in very physical or cognitive ways. In the intuitive style, the grievers talk about their feelings, emotions and emotional reactions.

These researchers also point out that there are some people who may lie in the middle and use a combination of both styles; these are referred to as blended grievers. They also talk about the dissonant grievers, whom they describe as, '. . . people who really experience grief one way but find it difficult to express it that way. This might be the male, who feels he has to maintain a strong image; though he's strongly intuitive in his experience, he does, in fact, repress his emotions.'

This is something which very often shows up in therapy. Saurin, a male client I worked with, who had lost his sibling, spoke about how he felt he had lost all his friends, since they kept telling him to 'man up'. This was in the first month, when they kept telling him to address financial and other logistical matters, while he found it hard to even get up and take a bath or eat his meals. He had lost weight and would cry in private—but in front of friends and family, he would remain quiet and withdrawn. Once, he told me, 'Therapy is the only place where I cry in front of someone else. My family believes that we need to accept and be strong. I can't be myself and it's hard to do that.'

Practical and Solution-Focused Grievers

A grieving style I began to see in my work very early on was how across gender, many people when surrounded by grief moved towards action. Folks, who are solution-driven in their grieving style, make sense of their grief by looking at what needs to be attended to. While a lot of media and literature associates this style primarily with men, in therapy sessions, I have seen a fair number of women across age groups as well, who prefer what I call 'The Solution-Focused Approach' to grieving.

Charmaine, a forty-four-year-old client, who I worked with in long-term therapy, told me, 'When I lost my dad, I was shaken and felt a sense of disbelief. However, I immediately moved towards attending to things that had to be done. I called my closest friends, who I knew had been through losses, and they immediately sent me numbers and volunteered to help me with the burial process and other logistics. My tears didn't flow till the time I was alone in my room that night. I spent the next few days helping my mum organize the house finances, bank details and figure out the living situation. I don't know if I'm suppressing my grief, as there are moments when I feel like crying and my grief comes in waves; more so in therapy sessions. Then, I go back to what needs to be done.'

These are people who deal with grief with an attitude of what needs to be done and solved. That doesn't mean they aren't feeling, or aren't not saddened by what's happening. It's just that their preferred style is to attend to what's emerging. Sometimes, they even perceive therapy as a solution to examine if they aren't dealing with emotions. This is what David Kessler talks about as the 'Practical Griever'. As he states, 'Some grievers don't talk about their loss, they don't cry a river of tears. They get back to normal as soon as they can.'

Learning to acknowledge that people have differing coping styles and ways of responding to grief is important. My experiences with clients tell me that people, who respond initially by jumping in to doing/solving things, are often judged and misunderstood as not feeling much or avoiding grief. Not just that—women are more likely to be judged for this style as compared to men. The unsaid expectation is that most women would respond to grief in an emotional way.

Emotional or Intuitive Grieving Style

Saumya lost her boyfriend during the second wave of the Covid pandemic. She reached out to me two months after the loss. She was inconsolable, her tears wouldn't stop and she had to pause multiple times before she could even complete a sentence. In her first session, she told me, 'I made notes, because I didn't know how I would be able to talk about Saurabh's death. I'm heartbroken and I can't get myself to stop crying. I wish I could just stop, but I can't manage to.'

Her coping style falls under what is referred to as the emotional or intuitive grieving style. She worked for a long time in therapy, unpacking each emotion that was emerging and dealing with the longing and yearning. She told me, 'The only way I can heal is by feeling and letting it go.' We did just that, gently and slowly, at the same time helping her with possibilities and ways that allowed her to get back to functioning and stepping in to a new world without her boyfriend, but one where her friends and family were there to support and be present for her.

Grieving Styles in the Age of Social Media

While grief is very private, in recent times, owing to the proliferation of social media, there is an increased pressure to be vulnerable when it comes to private moments. Very often, we judge people in relation to what we outwardly see when it comes to their grieving. We forget that an experience of grief is deeply personal. Using a lens of what is visible to outsiders for a process that's personal and private can often lead to unhealthy assumptions about how others are coping. This gets more difficult when we look at the grief of celebrities or public figures. While all public releases about death specify the need for privacy and respect in a moment of sadness, their grief gets judged. Their fame and status often cast such a shadow and, as a result, they don't get the privacy required and are at the risk of others making assumptions about their grieving process.

What we assume of people's lives or infer from social media is far from the truth. Grief is deeply private; even though there may be public posts, we can never really know how it's felt by the grieving individual.

Over the years, I have had clients tell me stories about their loved ones; and often, there is a retelling of the same stories. Now, when I look back at the last twenty years of my work, what I have come to realize is that frequently, grieving individuals come to therapy because their stories and memories aren't witnessed and heard in the ways they want it to be seen and listened to. Their grieving styles don't make sense to others and hence, they don't feel that their grief is understood or acknowledged. As Saumya mentioned, 'Losing my boyfriend was hard. But what's harder is coming to terms with the fact that everyone, including my own parents, have so quickly moved on. No one seems to engage with my memories emotionally. They don't ask me questions or share their memories and that breaks my heart. I wish they understood my grief.'

If there is one gesture that you can extend to someone who's grieving, it is to see their grief as they experience it and not impose your perspective or lens of moving on. I know it feels hard, but that's all they really need—an understanding and a witnessing.

19

Do We Really Recover?

The first few days of loss can be extremely disorienting and exhausting, where we have little or no energy to do much. As the rituals and ceremonies come to an end and relatives leave, we are left to ourselves and may begin to wonder, 'What happens to my life now?' Clients in therapy ask, 'Does the grief ever go away? It seems like I will never be able to do away with it. Will it always pain this much?'

There is no recovery or getting over grief. We learn to live with the grief and also hold space for love. We miss our loved one, who is no more with us, and we know that the world will never feel the same. At the same time, as we continue to do the work of dealing with our emotions, processing, accepting and integrating, our grief shifts. It stays, but it feels different.

As Anne Lamott says, 'You will lose someone you can't live without, and your heart will be badly broken, and the bad news is that you never completely get over the loss of your beloved. But this is also the good news. They live forever in your broken heart that doesn't seal back up. And you come through. It's like having a broken leg that never heals perfectly—that still hurts when the weather gets cold, but you learn to dance with the limp.'

As I pondered on the subject of this chapter, a statement that came to me instinctively was, 'Do we ever ask what happens to our love?' Just as love stays, grief stays. Grief is an extension of the love which we have felt for our loved one. Just because they have passed away, we don't stop thinking about them. We carry both grief and love in our hearts. I have found it useful to think that a huge part of processing our grief is acknowledging that the presence of our loved one felt like sunshine and hope. We were lucky to have them, and they made our world a better place. Now, when they are no more, we can make a choice to carry forward what they stood for, by imbibing qualities that we always associated with them. We can choose to celebrate them whenever life offers an opportunity. Personally speaking, my father was a huge foodie and loved exploring new cuisines. Over the years, on his birthday and death anniversary, I often order his favourite food—and while I am not a big foodie, I think I have become someone who savours the cuisine. All good food reminds me of him. Although I must mention that it has taken years to imbibe and see it this way, I'm glad it has happened.

We carry love and loss together.

As we continue processing our grief, it becomes integrated, and we begin to accept the loss. We start to recognize that our world has changed, and now one slowly needs to adapt to this new reality.

Early in therapy, clients often ask me these questions, and I have always felt that one can give hope and yet be honest with people. Truth and compassion can co-exist—my experience over and over has been that clients accept it well. As a young therapist, I thought it would be hard for them to hear this. But almost two decades later, I realize that grief is hard enough, and knowing what to expect realistically becomes an anchor, helping people rather than pushing them into a state of despair. I remember working with a seventy-year-old client, Naresh, who had reached out to me three years after the loss of his wife due to a chronic illness. He seemed quite agitated and distressed. He said to me, 'I have been to therapists and doctors, and everyone tells me that it's been three years and so, I must move on. I don't understand how I can move on and see life as the same. When the person I loved for fifty years is no more, everybody still wants recovery and wants me to be done with grief. It has taken me a lot to come here, and I don't think I can recover.'

I told him, 'You are right, there is no recovery from grief. No matter how much work you do with me, all I can help you is with grief integration and acceptance. Our grief is not an illness or condition that we can wish away. Your wife was your world and so, it will always hurt. Yet, we can work together to address what you are feeling. Perhaps we can move forward with her memories and the love that you hold for her.'

The client had tears in his eyes and said, 'That I can do. I have been doing that in my own way. Thank you for saying this. I needed to hear it. If you had promised recovery or said that I can get over grief, you know I would have never come back for another session.'

From a life standpoint, I feel that our grief shifts; life feels different, and things no longer are experienced as being the same. Yet, there is a possibility that people will find joy, happiness and excitement at some time, and sorrow, longing and yearning for our loved ones will continue to stay. In all those moments, we begin to accept that life feels bittersweet.

Many people, including my client, kept hearing that it 'gets better'. But the client didn't want things to get 'better', because better meant that they were forgetting all the love they had. So, 'better' was not what they needed.

Living with this truth is a huge part of the healing journey. The reality is that as we process the grief and it gets integrated, we find our own anchor within and learn that love can continue to exist, even after the loved one is gone. Our love finds a way and the legacy of the person continues to exist in ways we continue to love.

At the heart of grief lie important questions of how we choose to love, how we want to continue loving others, what values and beliefs we want to live by and ultimately, how do we live and build a good life, now that we recognize that life is limited. **Often, all grief work boils down to: 'How do I continue to live and love, now that I know loss is inevitable?' That's why I believe that how we deal with our grief is what determines how we choose to love, and even live our life.**

At the same time, I know that very early on in our grief process, this idea may not make sense. We make space for understanding in a way that's helpful. So, if doesn't make sense to you, choose to either let it marinate, discard it or stay with what makes sense to you.

Our life grows around grief, and at the same time, grief doesn't disappear. The intensity and sharpness of pain, as we continue to do the work of processing and integrating it, begins to shift. It begins to feel a bit less than what we experienced in the early days of the loss as we do the work of meaning-making and integration.

Yet, there are moments when the sharpness returns, and grief even after years feels like pain that never really left us. That is alright. This nature of grief is discussed in detail in the section on grief activators.

However, this process of grief integration requires both action and intention, and not just time. We need to do the work of finding a way to live with the loss and keeping the love intact, to start rebuilding our life all over again. As we do this, it will continue to feel unsettling at every step; and then, at some point in our grief journey, life will begin to make sense again, but in a different way. We will have the capacity to carry our love and grief and continue living our life.

20

Grief Activators

While there is no timeline to grief, both research and clinical experience show that predictable and unpredictable triggers are capable of evoking 'big feelings' in us all over again.

There are situations and occasions where the intensity of grief is heightened, and the grief still feels raw and fresh. Some of these occasions can be the first death anniversary, weddings, your own birthday, the birthday of the loved one who has passed away, social get-togethers, festivals and so on. Over the years, instead of using the term 'grief triggers', psychologists have moved to calling these situations 'grief activators.' This is a term that accurately captures how our grief gets reactivated. The intensity with which we experience it gets heightened and we feel the absence of our loved one much more in these specific moments. I have observed in therapy that clients begin to report anxiety and feeling tearful as they anticipate occasions that are a reminder of their loss. It's as if the anticipation of these 'big days' evokes feelings of absence, loss and sorrow. Personally, I have felt that even if I sometimes forget an important date that's a reminder of grief, my body seems to remind me. Some of these moments and occasions will continue to leave us teary-eyed, while also reminding us that we were loved . . . even years later. Over the years, I mindfully tell clients about this. If they find themselves in a space of feeling vulnerable, we choose to schedule sessions in the same week or on a day that reminds them of their loss.

There are also big milestone moments in our life, which are a reminder of how our life has moved on in some way, and might bring back memories of our loved one, who is no longer a part of it. Sumit, a week before his fiftieth birthday, told me, 'I can't believe that my mum is not here to wish me. We would often talk about how when I turned fifty, she would turn seventy-five that same year, and we would throw a party together. I miss her and feel so lucky to have received her love and unconditional acceptance.'

We all know there is always a restaurant, a holiday destination, old pictures, a song, a movie, or something else, all of which could bring old memories gushing back. Sudhir, a thirty-four-year-old male client, told me, 'Listening to a song that my wife and I danced to the first time at our wedding got me feeling overwhelmed. It has been five years since she passed away and, in that moment, it still felt so raw.'

We need to remember sometimes, even after years, we may experience intense sorrow and grief in these moments—that's okay.

On 1 May, my father's birthday, I once ordered dal pakwaan (a Sindhi delicacy) for the family. It had been nine years, at that point, since my dad had passed away. When I ordered it, it didn't consciously register that it was one of my dad's favourite meals. At the same time, as I began eating it, the childhood memories around my dad getting dal pakwaan from Chembur came back to me. In that moment I felt really fragile as I began eating. Over the years, I had processed the loss and was at peace, but the meal opened floodgates of emotion, where I really missed his presence, viscerally experienced a feeling of loss and thought about all the conversations we had never had.

What Helps

1. **An awareness of grief activators**: An understanding of grief activators often helps us make sense of our grief. This awareness can help the grieving individual pause and acknowledge what's arising, rather than be shocked by the intensity of what is felt.
2. **Giving oneself permission to feel:** Whether it's predictable or unpredictable occasions, we need to hold space for our own grief and embrace the fact that it's completely okay when this happens. The only way in these moments is to let the feelings run their course and let the tears flow. **Choosing to be compassionate** towards one's own self is crucial in these moments. Often, people judge themselves and slip into the space of beating themselves up for not being able to process and deal with the grief. It doesn't mean that you haven't processed or integrated the grief; in fact, it's a reminder that the love you felt continues to linger and the person you deeply cared for is no more around and hence feelings of loss are reactivated again.
3. **Be mindful of those big days and predictable triggers:** An attitude of mindfulness can sometimes help us be prepared for the feelings that may be evoked in us. A lot of clients, particularly the ones with an instrumental grieving style, feel that the vocabulary and science of grieving helps them deal with such days better.
4. **Figure out ways to mark the significant days:** Over the years, I have found it useful if clients can figure out a way to mark these important days consciously. This could be writing in a journal about what one is feeling or putting up a post on social media explaining what they are feeling. This in turn allows them to feel seen,

heard, understood and get support from others, which can be soothing. I have personally posted on social media about my grief. At the same time I have chosen to not have the comments option open, as I find it exhausting to respond.

Another way is to figure if you want to use that day to donate food, money or other things to a cause or NGO that is close to your heart or to your loved one, who passed away. My mum donates my dad's favourite food and makes a visit to the temple he used to really like going to both on his birthday and death anniversary. Over the years, I have also developed a practice of accompanying her to the temple. I feel a sense of comfort being there, and it feels like a part of him continues to be with us. I have had clients who choose to spend time at an orphanage or spend the day doing service, and that seems to soothe them.

For some people, the very act of taking time off from work and spending the day either by themselves or with friends and family also helps.

A client of mine would write letters every year to his brother who had passed away. It felt healing for him and a continuation of their shared connection.

5. **Soothing rituals, structure and seeking support**: These three 'S'es are in my view a necessary foundation that can help us in our grief journey, particularly when it comes to grief activators. As human beings, we are capable of self-soothing and engaging in rituals that allow us to feel anchored. Specifically on these days, it's a good idea to build time and engage in these rituals. This could be a workout, going for a walk, journalling, prayer, meditation or being with people

who are supportive and to whom you can talk about what's happening.

Both soothing rituals and then seeking out support intentionally go a long way in helping us feel less alone and dealing with feelings of anxiety, sadness and other emotions that may be consuming us. For a lot of people, it helps to have a structure and know what their day would look like. On some days when grief seems to come back in an intense way, people may feel confused, numb or have the desire to avoid the feelings that are evoked in them. As a result some people may engage in binge drinking, missing meals or working excessively to avoid the pain. I advise clients to become mindful if they tend to do this and, in turn, figure out a structure for their day. It also helps to become aware of which part of the day is when they need soothing rituals and support the most.

Sumit mentioned to me how evenings and nights are the toughest for him. So, we thought through it and at the end of the discussion, he decided that on his mom's death anniversary, he would either have friends over for dinner or spend time with them in the evening. He also informed them how he felt, so that it gave him a chance to be supported and not feel alone.

Saumya, whom we encountered in an earlier chapter on recognizing how vulnerable she feels on her birthday, decided that she would ask either her mum or her best friend to spend a couple of days with her. She feared that she would have sleepless nights and panic attacks, if she stayed by herself and their presence did help her to sleep and feel supported.

Recognize that it's normal for grief to emerge; learning to be self-compassionate to our own pain helps

All Those Moments When Grief Found a Way Back, When We Least Expected It

The nature of grief is sneaky, and it can show up in moments and situations when we least expect it.

Mahee, a seventy-five-year-old woman, told me, 'While coming to the clinic, I saw a bright red car. It reminded me of our first car, and I was left in a puddle of tears. My poor driver couldn't understand what was happening to me. It's been twenty years since my husband passed away, yet that passing car brought memories gushing back. How I miss him every day!'

Sometimes, hearing a voice that reminds you of your loved one or noticing books from their favourite author at a bookstore, and then on nights where you can't sleep, feelings of longing return, and tears may find a way back without us even realizing.

Activity

Take a moment to sit quietly with your eyes closed and write down when grief showed up for you in an unexpected manner. As you do this, allow yourself to sit with the feelings that are emerging. While writing this, if you find yourself crying or feeling overwhelmed, be gentle with yourself. Give yourself permission to feel and be mindful about not judging yourself.

Sometimes, all the love we feel finds its way into tears.

____

____

____

____

____

____

____

As I was writing and doing research for this chapter, I chanced upon this quote, and it really spoke to me.

> Memories are where our loved ones continue to live after they're gone; this is why we hold onto objects that remind us of them and go to places where they feel near. True, when someone we love dies, we are always at risk of their memory triggering aftershocks of the pain. But inversely, if we let them, such reminders may also fill us with warmth and comfort. In time you may even find that the very "grief triggers" that once caused you sadness now fill you with a sense of love and remembrance.[1]

I know that in the initial stages of loss, we may not feel comforted by these memories. As we do the work of processing and grief integration, some predictable and unpredictable moments become a space, a container into which our memories come back and remind us of how lucky we were to spend time with our loved one.

21

Addressing What Is Evoked in Us

We all deal with grief in our own way. Everyone I have worked with in therapy, friends and family, have all in their own time and through their own personal journey found a way to deal with grief. Although I do understand that in the first few days, and sometimes even months, after the loss, it feels like we are so broken that we will never be able to deal with it.

Clients often ask me what dealing with grief looks like. While the list is not exhaustive, here are some pointers that may help:

- Acknowledging various feelings that the loss evokes in you, including feelings like rage, relief, abandonment and so on.
- Learning to sit with the feelings and be able to articulate and talk about it.
- Allowing for social support and making space for vulnerability
- In our telling and retelling of stories, we begin to deal with grief.
- Slowly beginning to accept the loss.
- The work of personal meaning-making, which sometimes may happen in few months and then at other times, years after the loss.

- Reimagining and rebuilding our own life, in small and big ways, like developing a new morning routine, travelling alone for the first time after the loss and more.
- Reimagining one's own identity in the light of loss.
- Acknowledging that while grief stays, you may still be able to experience emotions that feel pleasant and life-affirming.
- Lastly, accepting that grief will stay and at the same time, we will continue to live with memories.

Activity

Take a moment to write down for yourself as you processed and began dealing with the grief, what did it feel like for you? It may help to look at the grief from a lens of cognitive, emotional, and physical symptoms described, and see what shifted and changed for you.

____
____
____
____
____
____
____
____
____
____
____

I remember a thirty-year-old client, Manya, who was in therapy soon after she lost her mum. We continued the grief work and one day, she told me, 'This is the first time in the sessions that I have been able to talk about my mum in the past tense. It's been almost five months to the loss and I'm beginning to feel that something has shifted. Maybe I'm beginning to accept that she is really gone.' The client had tears in her eyes. I remember asking her, 'What would your tears say in this moment?' The client said, 'My tears would say that there is a lightness. I feel guilty even stating it, but I suddenly think that I feel less burdened. I haven't been able to put the grief away and have been consumed with it. Today, in that moment when I talked about her as a memory, I felt happy thinking about her, and yet sad knowing that she's not around.'

As we do the work, the intensity of our feelings, and the frequency with which we experience them begins to shift. At the same time, there are grief activators that can bring back feelings with an increased intensity.

Over the years, as clients have done the grief work, here are some statements that they have used to describe what dealing with grief feels like:

- 'It still pains me, and the sadness and longing is there, but I don't cry all day.'
- 'I miss my partner, but I can regulate my mood much more easily.'
- 'It pains, but I can finally get myself to talk about my loss.'
- 'I know I was beginning to accept the loss, when for the first time I could talk about my brother in the past tense.'
- 'I accept that the grief will stay forever, and I can live with it.'
- 'It's becoming easier to live in the same house and I can now stay alone.'
- 'I no longer avoid meeting friends as I did in my early days of loss; I go out and have managed to even make new friends.'

- I feel that my brain fog has lifted; I can concentrate and focus better. I'm not as exhausted and feel ready to make decisions.'
- 'I finally feel ready to clear the cupboard and look at my dad's belongings. It's taken a year since he passed away, but I'm ready now.'

What I also see in therapy is that as clients begin to process and deal with grief, they begin to experience guilt. They begin to feel scared and wonder if they are forgetting their loved one. There is a sharp, critical voice that accompanies them even in moments of healing. Almost two years into therapy, Manya told me, 'In the last two sessions, I haven't mentioned my mum at all. We talked about other things. This morning, when I decided to make kheer, I fondly thought of her and missed her. At the same time, I panicked as I wondered if I was forgetting and losing all her memories. Is it fair to not be in pain? Shouldn't my heart continue aching?'

It's important we remember that love remains and continues to show up, and we don't need to beat ourselves up as we slowly process the grief.

While therapy is one of the ways in which people make sense of and deal with their grief, I don't think therapy is the only way. Therapy does help for some folks, who have the readiness and believe in the process. At the same time, spirituality and faith may help some people; others may find soothing and support in the form of friendships and family, who are there for them. Books, art, music and being in nature also contribute to a sense of healing and making sense of the loss. So, allow yourself to choose and work with what allows you to make sense of your grief.

22

Rebuilding a Life around Our Loss

Most of the time, when I have asked clients and friends about grief integration, there is always a smile; at the same time, their eyes well up because as they reply, they are reminded of how it has been a long and hard journey. The process of grief integration is an ongoing one. It can feel like there is a lightness that one begins to experience, and the intensity with which longing is experienced begins to shift, although the memories continue to linger.

Here are some statements that clients have shared over the years in sessions, reflective of the work they put in over time:

'It still hurts. I still miss my husband, but I can live with the loss. I can imagine falling in love with someone else and beginning life again.'

'The loss is a huge part of my life, but there is more to it than the loss.'

'I have learnt that memories will always seem bittersweet, and I can live with it.'

'I still watch our favourite movie for Diwali, but I have learnt to make new rituals and traditions. This year, I decided to go for dinner at my cousin's house and next year, I'm planning to invite them over.'

'I no longer feel bitterness, despair or think of myself as a victim. I have accepted the loss and I'm figuring out life all over again. It's hard but worth it.'

'I feel the ambivalence has shifted. I can forgive myself and also understand where my sister came from. I'm more at peace, not angry anymore.'

'I feel a sense of lightness; the gaping hole is no longer as big. The void seems to have been filled in a strange way.'

'Now, when I talk about my mum, I feel a sense of love and gratitude, rather than a feeling of grief over unfinished business.'

'The nature of my dreams of her have changed. They are no longer about abandonment.'

'The dreams are no longer about me drowning or everything falling apart. I can sleep peacefully.'

'I see my husband in my dreams, and it feels like he's continuing to be part of my life. He is just present, and I feel like he's watching over me, protecting me.'

'After eight years, this is the first time that I have told my best friend about my sister's suicide. No one other than you knew about it for the last two years. I feel lighter and my friend understood my pain.'

'I feel hope now. The helplessness and despair seem to be fading away.'

'I'm no longer fearful and anxious as I was in the first three years. I can make plans and I do think of my future with hope and enthusiasm in my heart.'

'I can allow myself to love others and even receive love. For a decade after my girlfriend died, I stopped myself from falling in love because it was a reminder that I would be hurt again, if I lose the person to death.'

Grief integration can look different for different people. For some, it is meaning-making by devoting their life to a cause.

For others, it is having the ability to share their pain with others when they would have chosen silence because of shame. Some may come around to accepting that life will remain bittersweet and learning to live with it. For some others, their dreams become a compass, indicating how their life has shifted. As you process the grief and it gets integrated, you will find your own anchor within and learn how your love can continue to exist, even after the loved one is gone.

Activity

Write down for yourself what grief integration felt like to you.

____

____

____

____

____

____

____

____

____

____

____

All the Conversations We Never Had

Grief, I feel sometimes, is a shapeshifter. With time, it seems to change its form and intensity, but also show up in ways that we least expect it to. We miss not just our loved one's presence, but also imagine what they would have said to us. We experience a yearning and helplessness in those moments. Our milestones are a continuous reminder of our grief and difficult moments, too.

Forty-one-year-old Snigdha, who lost her dad a few months ago, told me in a session, 'I often look at my daughter and wonder how my dad would have responded to her. I think of all the stories and anecdotes he would have told her, and then how proud he would have been of her. I grieve his loss, but I sometimes feel so bad that he didn't get to see her at all, and she was robbed of his love—a loss that my husband and my love can never make up for. Grandparents bring joy and unconditional love that parents can't offer.'

Snigdha and I talked about how she would like to introduce her daughter to her grandfather's memories. They started having a special storytelling time every Saturday, where Snigdha would tell stories that she grew up hearing from her father, and her daughter started calling it '*Naanu ki kahaaniyaan*'.

Often, in therapy, I ask clients to articulate and tell me the questions they would have loved to ask their loved one. As clients begin to share, they also start telling me possibly what their loved one, who has passed away, would have said. At other times, I encourage clients to speak to the deceased's friends and relatives, so that they can share stories, perceptions and even dreams. Some clients have shared in sessions how they continue writing emails and letters addressed to the deceased, and it feels like a conversation.

I never really got to ask my dad a lot of questions, since he spent so much time in and out of hospitals. Eventually, I did get in touch with one of my uncles and asked him what he remembered of my dad. That's when he shared how my father's dream was to write a book. This information made me feel connected to my dad and feel as if we shared a dream. So, if it helps, choose to get in touch with folks who knew your loved one, and you will be surprised with the answers you find.

Snigdha, a few sessions later, told me that the helplessness she felt from her grief was channelized into maintaining a personal diary for her daughter, where she started writing little details about her daughter, and nuggets of wisdom that she wants her daughter to have in case something happens to her.

23

Work and Relationships

Melanie, a twenty-nine-year-old woman in therapy, told me, 'My partner and I have been in a live-in relationship for the last three years. Around a year ago, he lost his mother due to kidney complications. Ever since then, our relationship has completely changed. I know that he loves me, but he is distant. There is barely any intimacy and I feel he has withdrawn. I'm scared that our relationship is falling apart. Does grief impact other interpersonal relationships, and is there a way out?'

This is a topic we don't talk about very often. At the same time, clients in therapy bring these concerns to address fears and anxieties about how their relationships changed in the light of grief.

Our personal identity is so much a result of the people we love. When we lose a loved one, we also lose a part of us. Most of the time, how we see the world around us and even our own self is impacted by the nature of our grief. That's why, after a loss, we may sometimes feel that others are responding to a part of us that no longer exists. This makes it hard for us to find a connection. As a result, it can bring about a distance or sometimes an end to already existing friendships or relationships, where either one feels misunderstood or struggles with unmet needs. Clients often come to therapy sessions to discuss how they feel so unsure about their relationships or marriage in the light of grief.

At the same time, grief can sometimes bring people closer and lead to deeper friendships and relationships. Then there are situations where grief can make us feel sure about a decision that has been pending or we have been on the fence about. I have worked with clients, who have decided to move countries or have a child soon after they experienced loss. These were all decisions they earlier didn't feel ready to make and felt uncertain about.

Activity

Take a moment to pause and think about friendships or intimate relationships in your life. If you have experienced loss, write down how and in what ways you have grown closer or distant from some of these people.

Tip: This exercise can evoke big feelings, so if you want to skip it, that's fine.

1. **How we grieve and mourn is so different:** When siblings, couples and families find themselves dealing with a common loss, how everyone grieves can look so different. These differences in coping and grieving styles can create a rift and misunderstanding. Mazhar and Sona were dealing with the loss of their unborn baby, as Sona had a miscarriage in her second trimester. Mazhar was grieving but found it hard to express what he felt. He told me in a session, 'All I feel is numb.' On the other hand, Sona couldn't stop crying. She was devastated and would weep for hours, to the extent that she had to be admitted in the hospital as she was neither eating nor sleeping. Sona couldn't understand Mazhar's response and felt that he didn't care at all. Mazhar struggled to understand the intensity with which grief showed up for Sona and felt that both were young and could try again to have a child. This led to massive altercations between them. When they reached out three months after the miscarriage, they mentioned how they were thinking of separation and were sleeping in different bedrooms as they couldn't stand each other.

   If we feel that our grief is not seen or understood by our family members, it can come in the way of relationships. Grief makes us fragile, vulnerable and at the same time, we are at the risk of feeling alone when our own partner, sibling or a parent doesn't understand our grief in the way we want them to. Often, without realizing, people in the same family dealing with the same loss end up judging each other for how grief is experienced, and this leads to friction and conflicts.
2. **How we want to be supported looks different:** After the miscarriage, Sona wanted to take time off from work, and spend time with Mazhar alone as she felt that

answering relatives and family was triggering her. Mazhar didn't want to be left alone with his own thoughts, so he fully immersed himself in work. He thought that work would allow him to feel less anxious. Sona wanted emotional comfort and soothing words; Mazhar, on the other hand, wanted practical advice. Both kept feeling that their needs were not met, and their grief was not seen. There is no right or wrong when it comes to how people want to be supported, yet if family members, couples or friends don't see eye to eye, it can make the grieving individual feel their emotional needs are unmet.

A client of mine, who lost her father suddenly to a cardiac arrest, told me how she felt abandoned by her close friend after her father's loss. She felt that her best friend didn't check enough on her and had become distant. As we discussed this, the client felt a desire to let her friend know about what she was feeling. My only advice was to do it in a gentle manner and face to face.

The client told her friend, 'I need more check-ins; this is the time I need us to be in touch more than usual, as I feel really fragile.' When she stated this, her friend mentioned how she was giving her space and had no idea that she required more checking in. Because the friend responded so beautifully to the feedback, they could repair the relationship and find support in a way that worked.

3. **Recognizing the inevitable nature of death and finding new meaning:** Sometimes, the death of a loved one is a reminder about one's own mortality and as a result, a compelling force that propels people to lead a more meaningful life.

Losing a loved one to death in a strange way offers us perspective on our life. As Irvin Yalom, a well-known psychoanalyst, says, 'Though the physicality of *death* destroys *us*, the idea of *death* may *save us*.'

Daryl, a forty-year-old client, told me, 'My best friend died of a heart attack. His death has shaken me. I began to realize that the stress in his job impacted him and all his dreams of accomplishing purposeful work are gone. I now want to put in my papers and start working on my passion project, whereby I can help children with education, and work in rural areas.'

Amidst all the pain and sorrow, some people begin to see things clearly, and everything suddenly makes sense. This, in turn, becomes the fuel for making life-changing decisions, like it did for Daryl, who in a year after his friend's death quit his job, opted for a slower pace of life and moved to a quieter part of the country, where he is surrounded by nature and can directly work with children.

At the same time, I have worked with clients, who soon after losing a loved one feel the need to tie the knot or commit to a relationship. Suddenly, milestones, companionship and legacy assume new meaning.

Having said that, one needs to be mindful about the factors that shape our decisions. Grief can be a powerful force and it's important to sit and realistically evaluate life decisions before making a big transition. Becoming aware of our own potential for impulsive decision-making can help us to make more informed choices. A good idea is to allow ourselves a time frame before we make the decision. Learning to discern what's driving the decision is crucial. Our values, emotions, impulses, anxiety, fears and then a gut feeling—all of these can push us towards decision-making. So, becoming aware of this can help us make a realistic evaluation and, in turn, make an informed choice.

4. **The fear of death and death anxiety:** Suchi, a thirty-four-year-old woman in therapy, shared, 'It's been two years since my mother-in-law passed away. My life and marriage have changed since then. My mother-in-law was healthy and exercised regularly. When we were on a holiday, she had a heart attack and died on the spot. It was a huge shock to all of us and we were all heartbroken. A couple of months after her loss, my husband became obsessed with his health and weight. He started worrying that he would die of a heart attack, too. We have been to cardiologists in India and abroad, but the fear and anxiety continue to haunt him. Our cardiologist recommended a therapist as he felt that it was turning into hypochondria, but my husband doesn't believe in the therapy process. I love him dearly, but I can't be constantly reassuring him. I feel that the last two years have exhausted me, and I don't know if I want to be in this marriage. I'm scared and don't want to take a hasty decision.'

   There are times when the death of a loved one can leave family members with an all-consuming fear of mortality. If this fear is persistent and intense, it can take the shape of lingering anxiety or hypochondria, which can then impact the person's relationships, work and most importantly, quality of life. If the death of a loved one has evoked a fear of death in you that is intense and ongoing, it's a good idea to work with a mental health professional. While it's common for fear to be evoked, if it continues to linger and takes the form of intrusive and obsessive thoughts, choose to attend to it. The process can help you address the unrealistic beliefs and fears that grief may have evoked in you. The therapy process can help in cultivating realistic beliefs, address hypervigilance and help with acceptance, when it comes to recognizing the fragility of life.

Often in therapy, when clients seem to be in a rush to end long-standing relationships or make a hurried decision about having a baby, I suggest that clients do both individual and couple work. This becomes a way to process what they are feeling and not make hasty decisions.

Grief changes us and our interpersonal relationships. Being aware of this and making the time to work though what's happening to us, how we relate to the world and to our partners is crucial before we take any big decisions.

24

You Are More than Your Grief

When we are grieving, people first look at our grief and then us. This somehow changes the way we feel seen, heard and how we are hosted.

Pia, a thirty-two-year-old client in therapy, told me, 'It's strange how people look at me. I lost my parents in a tragic accident, which you know. But for more than six months now, it's as if that's the only part of my life people want to acknowledge or see. I have understood in therapy that grief continues to live on, and memories of loss will keep getting evoked. At the same time, when I'm reduced to people seeing me only through this lens and pitying me, I feel grief has become my own identity. When I joined office a month later, everyone was so silent around me. They had sent messages to me and expressed condolences, but their silence and not involving me in regular conversation felt so isolating, and a reminder of grief.'

This is something that keeps coming up in therapy sessions. It becomes more pronounced particularly when the death has happened due to unfortunate circumstances. For people, whose loved one was popular and, in the spotlight, their family members may feel that their identity becomes just about the loss; it's hard for people to see them for who they are.

Clients in therapy often talk about how the society views them and their pain. The reactions can range from a culture of silence at workplaces and schools to the gaze that feels like pity, all making the grieving individual feel that their loss has become their identity. This lens of being seen with sympathy creates very little space for people to be themselves and, most importantly, comes in the way of grief integration.

We discussed how friendships get impacted in the aftermath of grief, but it's common for grieving clients to talk about how when they begin to head out for social occasions, people become silent around them and conversations pause. Sumi, a sixty-one-year-old woman, who lost her husband, told me in a session, 'My husband was ill, and we knew that he was going to die. Yet, after he passed away, things have changed socially. I just feel like my friends treat me differently. I can't understand if they don't know how to deal with me or my grief. There is more to me, and no one seems to remember that.'

Hearing her comment reminded me of Nora McInerny, an author and podcast host. In a TED Talk, she says, 'I'm just trying to do what I can to make more people comfortable with the uncomfortable, and grief is so uncomfortable. It's so uncomfortable, especially if it's someone else's grief.'[1]

Maybe we really don't know how to speak or be around people who are grieving, either because it triggers our own fears of loss, or unconsciously we start seeing them only through the lens of loss. As a result, when people go back to work after their bereavement leave, they worry about how they will be received, and the conversations that others may possibly have or sometimes not have. What clients tell me is that they want others in office to check in, but also include them and keep conversations going as they generally would. As Pia mentioned to me, 'I wish people around me would trust the fact that if I'm overwhelmed or uncomfortable with a topic, I can soothe myself and even step out. I want people to stop tiptoeing around me and act like they earlier would. The awkward silences make it seem like now I need to work hard at making them feel comfortable, although I'm the one grieving.'

We as a society need to become sensitive to when we hold space for the bereaved individual and when not be nosy and intrusive. Ronit, a thirty-three-year-old, who lost his wife to cancer, mentioned to me in a session, 'After my wife's loss, everyone is only interested in my love life and focused on helping me get a partner. When I was in my early days of grief, I sensed an attitude of pity and sympathy, which I hated. It seemed like I was looked upon as this "person whom life has been unfair to, who needs to be rescued". I could sense an attitude of pity in people's eyes when they looked at me. Now, it's been three years since she passed away, I miss her every day, but I moved cities, changed jobs and got back to a routine. Still, when I meet cousins, acquaintances and old friends, all they can talk about is my wife and how I should move on. They seem to not be interested in anything beyond that and it makes me feel sad and angry at the same time.'

While in India, we see ourselves as belonging to a collective culture, it's important that we respect people's boundaries and check with them whether they are comfortable or not, when it comes to discussing certain private matters.

We owe grieving individuals an attentive presence and witnessing, along with empathy that allows them to feel included and not singled out because of their loss. Ultimately, there isn't anyone who will never experience loss; all of us either have or eventually will.

Part 4

The Way Forward

25

Sorting through the Deceased's Possessions

Should I Be Clearing the Cupboard?

Malini, who was thirty-three, reached out to me for therapy. In the first session, she spoke about how, two years previously, she had lost her father due to a routine procedure gone wrong. In our first session, she mentioned, 'I have decided to rent out my dad's house. It has been over two years since his death, but I haven't touched his cupboard or any of his belongings. Now, the idea of giving his house on rent means that I must sort through his cupboard, which I have been avoiding. I can't get myself to think about it or do it. The act of emptying it out means acknowledging that he's gone. I even thought of not giving the house on rent and that's when my friend suggested that I reach out.'

Malini was married and lived in the same city as her late father. But after his demise, she had chosen not to enter the house. Going there and seeing the home without her dad used to make her feel nauseous, dizzy and she would start crying inconsolably.

This is one of the topmost concerns that comes up when clients are dealing with grief and even when they are anticipating a loss.

While paperwork and finances can be sorted out with either an estate lawyer or bank officials, the act of going through and emptying a cupboard of the possessions of the deceased is something that the immediate family member(s) must look into. One can involve friends and family to make these calls, but the final decision is yours. It's a hard task at every level as it evokes feelings of isolation, sorrow and pain all over again.

This gets further complicated if the deceased has multiple properties and a habit of storing stuff for years and not sorting it out. Then, the loved one is left with the arduous task of spending weeks, even months, trying to make decisions. The process can seem daunting, scary and anxiety-provoking, given the yearning and pain it evokes

Some clients have shared that the act of sorting felt like re-experiencing the early days of loss. Then, there are other clients who have talked about it as a process that allowed them to experience closure and move on. Other clients talked about how this process became a ritual that allowed them to celebrate the deceased's life, their memories, and at the same time say a final goodbye.

One of the questions that grieving individuals keep asking is 'When should I clear the house, cupboard and belongings?'

The short answer is: There isn't a fixed time.

Long answer: While there isn't a rule or guideline around it, I have worked with clients and know of families who have struggled and have chosen not to clear a cupboard for years, or even look at it. In most cases, there is either delayed grief that's been at work or overwhelming situations, either positive or negative, that haven't allowed family members to get to this point. Then, there are people who have done it in the first month itself, sometimes even in the same week. In fact, I can tell you from personal experience, when my father passed away, we sorted through his stuff within a month of his demise. At that point, the grief was so overpowering that even looking at the room in which he spent most of the time when he was bedridden was a reminder of his absence. Now, when I think about it, I feel if I had given myself more time, there were some things I associated with him that I would have liked to have kept, or even shown to my daughter, who barely got to know him.

Since this is a realization, I have had almost ten years after he passed away, I always tell my clients that when grieving and in doubt, allow yourself to not immediately jump into the cleaning and sorting. While there isn't an appropriate time to do this—because it will always remain hard—choose to do it slowly if that's what you have the energy for. When you are unsure, like in the first month, it's okay to not do it right away. Trust what feels right for you.

I know many people who feel that they have experienced chronic stress from 2020 onwards, which hasn't allowed some of them to spend their resources and energy into this task of 'clearing the cupboard'. So, you need to be gentle and mindful as you step into this process. At the same time, pause and examine if you are choosing to avoid doing it for too long.

Here are some pointers that may help you as you look at either a full house or one that contains the belongings of your loved one:

1. **Acknowledge that it's hard:** No matter what your relationship is with the deceased, whether it's intimate or ambivalent, the process of emptying the wardrobe and the room can be very hard. If it feels overwhelming, know that you are not alone. Everyone I know and have worked with has talked about it. If your loved one slowly chose to donate their stuff or made a list about where it all needs to go, the process does get a little easier. However,

when there aren't clear instructions given about how to dispose of the stuff and how it needs to be allocated or distributed, the process of clearing gets difficult

A friend mentioned how her dad had chosen to declutter and simplify his life in his sixties and had told her who his things should go to in case of his death. He also wrote a note saying that if any of his children want to take some of his belongings, they could choose when he was alive so that things were easier and sorted out in his presence.

2. **Doing the sorting all by yourself can be very difficult:** As I write this, I realize it's an understatement. It can be devastating because as you look at the stuff left behind, you are constantly reminded of the loved one's absence and the fact that you will never see them again. Ask for support, whether it's from friends, family members or your staff; let someone be with you in the same room. Allow them to stay with you during the process. Remember that people who care and love us deeply may not know or understand how and when we need support in difficult times. So, make an active call to articulate your need. I tell clients to sort things into three distinct piles: what they know needs to be thrown away, what needs to be kept and what they are unsure about.

   If you choose to donate the stuff, it may still be okay to ask a friend to accompany you and be with you as you give it away. The reality is that even after you have made up your mind to give these things away, it is still painful to let them go.

   There is a huge possibility that as you choose to give away the items, you realize that there are so many belongings you don't know what to do with. Most clients I have worked with have felt unsure and, as a result, the process of sorting is something they have done in parts or left midway, because they can't bear to sit through it. This process is particularly hard in cases where there is a full house or family home that needs to be sorted, since it belonged to a deceased person who lived alone.

When in doubt, a good idea is to get boxes/cartons where you can put away the stuff you want to give away perhaps to a charity, the items you want to discard in another box/boxes, and then one separate box or boxes for stuff you are unsure about, which you can come back to in some weeks or a few months to look at and assess your choices.

Things like medicines, toothbrushes, dental care kits, etc. are easier to take care of. Then, there are belongings that are hard to part with—like a shirt that you loved, a book that your parent was fond of, a bag that they saved up all their money to buy or perfumes that remind you of their scent, which feels so familiar.

3. **Too many claimants:** Sometimes, grief gets harder when there are arguments or claims made by family members over the things left behind. How odd is it that nobody tells us how, as we continue to deal with our grief, the desire to possess the stuff of our loved one may exist in others. It's hard to wrap our heads around this, but it could happen.

   Rishabh, a twenty-eight-year-old, lost his wife in an accident. He told me, 'After my wife passed away, I was in a state of shock, and felt that I was moving from one day to another like a zombie. Right after the thirteenth day ceremony, my wife's sister asked me what I was planning to do with her clothes and bags. I told her that I had not thought about it. She told me that since I'm dealing with so much, she would take this upon herself. Since her clothes size is the same as my wife's, she would take the shoes and clothes. I was numb when I heard this. She opened the cupboards and began sorting and picking out the items she wanted. I felt betrayed and disgusted. I didn't want to keep any of it, but it made me wonder if thirteen days was what it took for your own sibling to grieve and move on.'

Therapy sessions over the years have been full of stories like this—whether it is sarees, bags, watches, suitcases or sneakers, and even more stories when expensive designer items were left behind. The timing, pace and how things are managed can have an impact on how betrayed, hurt, manipulated and angry the bereaved individual feels.

4. **Give yourself permission to work at your own pace**: As someone who's grieving, make a conscious choice to take time and pick a pace that works for you. It's not prudent to keep delaying it, so set a timeline to sort through stuff, and when you feel uncertain, keep a box that you can go back to, to figure what you need to do with it.
5. **Converting the stuff left behind into a memoir**: A friend once told me how she used some of her father's shirts and turned them into a blanket, a reminder of him and his life. Some clients over the years have chosen to keep a sweater, hoodie or turned possessions into accessories as a reminder of the person they loved.

Even though we may do the work of sorting and giving away, grief remains. The reality is so much of our own belongings, clothes and accessories continue to remind us of the person who is no more. Rishabh, as we continued to do the work, told me two years

> down the line, 'Every time I wear this white linen shirt, I'm reminded of my wife. She would love this shirt and would always comment on how it fitted me so well and how handsome I looked. I haven't told this to anyone, and this is the reason I avoided wearing this shirt. Now, I choose to wear it, and on those days, it feels like I'm carrying a part of her with me. While I have given away all her stuff, and some has been taken away by her sister, what am I supposed to do with my own clothes, which constantly remind me of her? My cupboard is filled with shirts and ties that she gifted to me. It's been years, and I can't seem to figure out what to do.'

To share such tender, personal moments is not easy, as clients worry they will be judged for still holding on and being too emotional, particularly when some time has passed since the loss. As a result, often, therapy is the space where they articulate these concerns. While grief gets integrated as we do the work of processing and making sense of it, our love remains. Whether it's a song, a restaurant one regularly visited or clothes, they are a reminder of time shared, which one can't get back. Our grief is ultimately a reminder of all the love we have to offer, knowing that the person who we deeply cared is no longer with us to receive it.

26

Grieving in a Digital Age

Malini tells me, 'It's been two years and I have kept my dad's phone with me. I keep going back to the WhatsApp chats we shared and re-reading them. Holding on to his phone is a reminder that he's still there. Earlier, I told myself that I need his phone for the bank work but now I feel that I'm holding on to it. I even end up calling up the number sometimes and then it hits me—he's no more. Do you think it's time to let it go?'

Technology at large has changed how we experience grief. Dealing with loss is complicated enough, and now we must figure out another layer, which is technology and grief. Sometimes, technology makes it easier for us to process things, allowing us to make meaning and even find comfort as we use it to deal with our grief.

At other times, the very presence of technology makes it harder for us to let go; it is a continuous reminder of the loss. This is true for grief of all kinds, not just when we lose a loved one to death. When a relationship ends, for instance, clients often talk about how they find it difficult to manage their loss in the digital age, where there are continuous virtual reminders of togetherness and the love that was shared.

We are living in a world now, where whether we like it or hate it, we need to start figuring out how we can grieve in the digital age. Rishabh, who had lost his wife, told me how social media reminders about their shared times together were a trigger for him. Particularly when he saw these the first thing in the morning in the first three months following the loss, he would feel nauseous, unable to breathe and would spend all day feeling immense sorrow. Finally, he decided to save all the pictures, but deactivate the accounts after a few months.

Grieving in a Digital Age

The reality is that the same experience can mean different things to different people. So, when it comes to technology, learning how it impacts your own grief is crucial. At the same time, hasty decisions should be avoided, because once accounts are closed, they can't be retrieved, phone numbers given away can't be claimed back and the same is true for email addresses as well.

For most people I have worked with, what I have understood is that we end up having an ambivalent relationship with technology in matters of grief. It's something we figure out as time passes by**. To each their own, specifically when it comes to technology.**

When Technology Serves a Purpose

My mother often finds soothing and solace in listening to my grandmom's voice recordings. She says that technology has made the process of grieving a little easier. Hearing her mother's voice makes her feel calm and more at peace.

Rishabh told me how some of his wife's colleagues and friends using social media platforms reached out to him and shared stories of her kindness and compassion, which showed him another beautiful side of her. He said that while he feels blessed that technology allows for all of this, he also kept feeling overwhelmed by these interactions as they demanded energy. He had never even met some of these people who reached out, and he wasn't sure after a point how much energy he needed to be investing.

I often ask clients to think about moments in which technology is helping them with their grief, and what aspects of technology are not serving a purpose when it comes to their own feelings.

When Technology Doesn't Serve a Purpose

On some days, it can feel like every time you are beginning to catch a breath or take a new step, the digital landscape reminds you of an old memory, and you slip back into sadness all over again. Malini felt that she was comforted by reading the message exchanges that she and her dad had shared but at the same time, the calls she made to the number left her feeling anxious and stuck in a pattern of denial. A few sessions in, I asked her how often she made these calls daily. She said, 'At least twice a day, and on days when I'm stressed and missing him a lot, it is ten to twelve times. I want it to stop, but it feels obsessive.'

The calls were leaving her exasperated and sometimes after making them, she would cry for hours.

Myra, who lost her older brother to cancer, told me, 'I was having a good day, feeling hopeful about my new job, and suddenly Google Photos shows me memories from five years ago, when my brother was still alive. As soon as this happened, my mood changed and I felt a wave of grief and despair. Don't get me wrong, I still love my brother and he's a part of my life. But I hate it when technology becomes a reason for my grief re-surfacing. It feels sneaky and I lose all control. I feel all my hope dissipate.'

A year after my father's death we gave away his phone and his number. I still remember in 2020 on Telegram as a part of notifications, I got a message saying, 'Papa joined Telegram'. My heart skipped a beat, and I had an immediate urge to call the number. I had made sense of the loss, even integrated it to large extent, but it shook me for a few days. I even called my mum to ask if we had really given away the phone. Finally, in 2020, I deleted the number. The act of deleting it felt hard and like I was letting go of a part of him that I shouldn't. I strangely wondered for long whether I should just keep it.

The reality is that grief feels so sneaky anyway, and on some days, I wonder if technology makes it sneakier.

When Technology Reveals Secrets

A sixty-seven-year-old male client, Nikhil, told me, 'A couple of months after my wife passed away due to a heart attack, as I was clearing her emails, I came across a trail of mails shared between my best friend and her from ten years ago. These emails were deep and intimate, indicating a strong emotional relationship, which I had no idea of. Now both are dead, and I'm stuck with this suspicion that maybe they had an affair that I never knew of. I don't know what to do. I still want to think of my wife as someone who loved me and whom I loved back, but now I must work through the trauma of possible infidelity. Should I possibly ask my best friend's wife if she knew anything about them, or am I complicating things for her? I'm feeling stuck and obsessed with this now, and I can barely sleep.'

We need to begin acknowledging that technology can complicate our grieving process, and, at the same time, it can help us find some calm in difficult moments. As a result, some people want to hold on to it and others want to just completely let go.

Having said that, how we navigate grief in a digital age is a choice we need to make. Learning to figure out your own personal relationship when it comes to tech and grief is an important part of the grieving process in today's times. A good idea is to spend some time observing how technology is affecting you when it comes to grief. What technology and the presence of gadgets will evoke in you in the aftermath of loss is hard to predict with certainty.

When the loss has just happened, it's not a good time to make big decisions about your loved one's phone or social media accounts. Give yourself time to figure things out and examine how you want to do it. Given that we live in an age where many important documents are linked to a phone number or email, you may need to be mindful about the phone and email addresses of your loved one.

If you are someone who's a practical griever, you need to be patient and remember that the act of waiting and figuring out what is to be done eventually is also an action step. Learn to be gentle and not rush into decision-making.

27

All the What-Ifs

Sasha, who is thirty-one, told me in a session while crying inconsolably, 'I keep going over and over the day it happened. I wonder what if I had gone to the gynaecologist a day earlier, or what if I had not gone for that walk before the bleeding started. Maybe I would have still had the chance to save my pregnancy. I just can't stop thinking about this and while I know it is obsessive, it's hard to stop the re-playing.'

Rajan, a sixty-nine-year-old whose wife passed away, said, 'I keep thinking how it would have been better if I had died instead of her. She never smoked or drank and exercised every day. Forty years of healthy life and now she is gone. It's unfair that I'm alive and she is not. In all my dreams, I keep imagining that I'm dead and she is still there. I wish I could just do that.'

Grief at its very core leaves us broken and with an absence that we can't do anything about. This helplessness leaves us with what-if and if-only scenarios. Every client dealing with grief engages in this process. These are part of the grieving cycle and Elisabeth Kübler-Ross, has a name for this. She calls this 'bargaining', which is explained in an earlier chapter. Bargaining in some way is an extension of denial, which is also a stage of grief.

As a therapist, in my experience, these what-ifs come tinged with a feeling of guilt, anxiety, sadness and helplessness, and assume various forms.

1. **All the 'what-ifs' about what could have been done**: Very often, after a difficult diagnosis of life-threatening illness or an accident, the what-ifs show up. Like one client with Stage 4 cancer diagnosis told me, 'If only I had gone for the check-up earlier, maybe the cancer would have not spread so much.' These what-ifs also show up for the caregiver at various stages, where they keep wondering if they hadn't given their loved one timely care, or frequently think about the cues they possibly missed.

   These what-ifs also raise their head when someone passes away, and family members often replay the scenarios in their head back and forth to make sense of the loss, particularly when the death is sudden or because of an accident. These negotiations come from a space where the caregiver keeps feeling that the death could have been avoided.

   One client told me, 'I keep thinking what if the doctor had reached the highway earlier after the accident took place; maybe my husband would have survived.'

   These are our ways of trying to feel that in some way, we could have controlled the outcome and, in turn, changed it.
2. **The 'what-if' and 'if-only' as a way of negotiating with God**: While all 'what-if' and 'if-only' scenarios play out specifically in our head, this one is very personal. As Dr Elisabeth Kübler-Ross and David Kessler mention in the book, *On Grief and Grieving*, 'After the loss, these what-ifs take the place of a

temporary truce.'[1] People who believe in God, spiritual healers or priests often go to the place of worship and engage in a barter that can be of two types:

a. **Hoping that their life is/was taken:** It's very common for caregivers to engage in 'what-if' and 'if-only' scenarios, in which they wish that their loved one had survived and their life was taken instead.

   When the death happens due to accidents or homicide, the surviving person might find themselves thinking about how their life should have been taken, too. Such an 'if only' can come tinged with survivor guilt in set-ups where a loved one passed away and others were rescued, escaped or were spared.

b. **Choosing to engage in a specific action or forgoing an activity or pleasure that one enjoys:** Aman, a forty-six-year-old client, told me that for the longest time, he hadn't gone to the temple. Then. when his mother fell seriously ill, he ended up going there every day and praying for her. He told me, 'I have been told that when you ask something for a loved one, you should keep it to yourself. I haven't told this to anyone, but I have decided that if my mum makes it through the surgery, I will give up eating non-vegetarian food and alcohol for all my life. If someone had told me this a few months ago, I would have found this barter so unrealistic. But I'm so desperate now and want her back, so this is the least I can offer.'

   If you have also, silently in your head, made similar truces or barters, it's understandable. The loss or possibility of loss leaves us feeling so shaky that we often begin to find a sense of grounding by holding on to such thoughts. In a strange way, all these what-ifs are our way of finding hope and at other times, a way of dealing with our helplessness and guilt.

3. **What-ifs about the future:** These are about the moments that the person who passed away would not get to see or be part of. The fact that someone whom you dearly loved is no longer going to be part of the future you envisioned can be devastating. This sadness can feel all-consuming, and more so when there are occasions or momentous milestones, the what-ifs are preceded by a feeling of longing. This specific kind of 'what-if' can seem the most challenging, even when it comes to articulating what one is feeling. Urvashi, a sixty-five-year-old client, had been working on her book for months. Her sister was a huge part of the journey, supporting and being a major cheerleader for her. A month before the book came out, her sister passed away due to a silent heart attack. When the book was finally published, Urvashi told me, 'I feel happiness and sorrow at the same time. My sister, who is part of this book and the reason I could finish writing, is no longer with us. I wonder what she would have felt, and how we would have shared this moment together.'

   These are moments when we need to be tender towards ourselves. It's a time to mindfully extend self-compassion and remind ourselves that as humans, we are capable of holding mixed feelings. It's okay for us to experience two opposite emotions at the same time. In these moments, I hold space for clients to express what they are feeling and remind them that happiness and sadness can co-exist.

Our what-ifs in these moments are about yearning for our loved one's presence and sitting with their absence. Learning to acknowledge and honour this bittersweet feeling is a huge part of grief integration.

Grief Math

I read about this term for the first time in an article written by Eleanor Haley, titled, '"How Old Would She Be Now?" and Other Grief Equations'.[2]

Most people I have known and the clients I have worked with have engaged in this process of 'Grief Math'. This shows up in small and big ways—we find ourselves thinking how old our parent would have been if they had been alive, counting the number of weeks it has been since we lost the loved one, and so on. Grief Math finds a way to show up particularly around birthdays, anniversaries and important milestones.

Grief Math is a way of fondly thinking about our loved one and imagining how their life would have shaped up. It is also a way of acknowledging the loss and how our lives would have felt together.

I have seen both young children and adults engage in this. When this happens, create a space for people to talk about what they are feeling. Sometimes, in our urge to protect people we love; we unconsciously or consciously change the topic and try to distract them. I don't think that's a good idea, because we are indirectly telling them that we don't want to listen to this, or that it's not okay to talk about this.

The Dangers Attached to What-If and If-Only

The stages of grief are non-linear and every person, who has lost a loved one, ends up engaging in 'what-if' at some point. At the same time, if these 'what-ifs' become intense and obsessive, they can become anxiety-provoking. A client once told me, 'I haven't been able to sleep for ten days as I keep thinking about what I could have done differently to save my partner. I wonder if I chose the right doctor, the right hospital and if I missed any cues. Even when I sleep, all my dreams are all about making mistakes and people losing their life as a result. I really need this to stop; I feel like I have begun to hate myself.'

This degree of obsessiveness and consistent rumination evokes anxiety, but also triggers low moods and at times is combined with feelings of despair and self-loathing. There are other times when the thoughts around what could have been done differently and 'if only' become so overwhelming that the surviving person finds it hard to function and harbours suicidal ideas. In all these moments, it's very important to work with a mental health professional, understand the intensity and frequency of these 'what if' statements/thoughts and assess how much they impact the person's day-to-day functioning, productivity and even self-esteem. Sometimes, when the thoughts are obsessive and, in turn, lead to severe depression or apathy towards oneself, a combination of psychiatric medication and psychotherapy is recommended.

If you find yourself engaging in bargaining, here is what you can do:

a. **Choose to give words to it and put it down on paper:** I suggest to clients that they maintain a grief journal. Writing and putting things down on paper can help us in breaking through the ruminative pattern, which is a danger that comes with bargaining. In my experience, as people begin to write things down, they sometimes can see through their own irrational thoughts. They start noticing how they may be discrediting all that the doctors and oncologists have said; during the writing process, they start integrating those experiences and coming to terms with the reality of the event. Writing may or not work for everyone, so be mindful as you begin to engage in this.

b. **Choosing to process the feelings that underlie bargaining:** In my experience, what generally lies behind bargaining is a myriad of feelings. These feelings may not be just about the incident, but also the kind of relationship that one has shared with a loved one before their demise. These feelings could range from sadness to helplessness, shame or even guilt about the way they may have treated a loved one. A client had stopped speaking to a sibling for ten years. After the sibling's demise, he told me, 'I keep thinking about how my sister would have not suffered as much if only I was there to take care of her and was present at the hospital.' Learning to acknowledge our feelings and even addressing them could be another way we can deal with the what-ifs.

c. **Hindsight bias:** When it comes to grief and trauma, very often people engage in what we call 'hindsight bias'. Hindsight bias is, according to the *APA Dictionary of Psychology*, 'The tendency, after an event has occurred, to overestimate the extent to which the outcome could have been foreseen. Hindsight bias stems from (a) cognitive inputs—people selectively recall information consistent with what they now know to be true; (b) metacognitive inputs—people may misattribute their ease of understanding an outcome to its assumed prior likelihood; and (c) motivational inputs—people have a need to see the world as orderly and predictable.'[3]

As a therapist, what's most important is to recognize and discern when to introduce this term to the client

> who is grieving. Various factors, such as the readiness of the client, the conditions under which death took place and many other conditions determine how this concept can help a client. An understanding of this bias allows people to be kinder towards themselves and even see through their own blind spots.

All the what-ifs are a reminder of our loss. As one continues doing the inner work, we slowly begin to realize that what-ifs are our way of feeling control and hoping that the loss could be averted in some way.

28

Secondary Losses

> **Reading Instructions**
>
> I would suggest that you read this chapter slowly, in parts. If you find it overwhelming or triggering, please choose to pause and return to it when ready. If you feel that you just need to skim through the chapter and move to the activity to identify the secondary losses you are experiencing, that's fine, too. Trust what your body tells you. The idea is you know what works best for you.

Shobha, after her mum's loss shared, 'What makes grief harder are all the losses that come in the aftermath of grief—where disappointment, abandonment and even disillusionment kicks in. My mum was the glue that kept the family together. When she passed away, my aunts were there for the cremation and the rituals. But it's as if they forgot to check in with my father and me. It's been two months since she passed, and they haven't visited us. They stay just fifteen minutes away. When mum was around, she would make sweets for everyone, and they would be home at least a couple of times in a month. To add to this, one of my friends, whom I was close to, never came at all for two weeks. I don't know how to make sense of all this. On some days, I feel more angry and bitter about these losses than my mum passing away. Am I being selfish in the way I'm grieving?'

The grief we experience is a culmination of the primary loss, losing our loved one to death, and then many secondary losses that add up.. What Shobha was talking about are losses that each one of us has experienced in some way. While they are known as secondary losses, the term doesn't do full justice as it gives the impression that they are less painful. The simple explanation is that since the loss of a loved one to death is considered a primary loss, all the related concerns that follow the demise of the person are labelled as secondary losses.

Commonly Experienced Secondary Losses

In the section below, I have tried to describe some of the secondary losses that show up very often for most people who are grieving.

1. **Change in social relationships:** A friend once told me, 'I don't know anyone who, in the aftermath of grief, hasn't lost a friend.' We both smiled at each other as for most people we know, and for a lot of my clients in therapy, dealing with grief has also meant dealing with disappointment, the absence of calls or check-in from friends, siblings, relatives and people who really matter. A physical absence and then lack of concern often changes the entire fabric of relationships. It's common for clients to bring up their disappointment and feeling of abandonment. They wonder if they over-invested in some relationships. People who lose a partner, for instance, talk about how they feel like an odd one out when they hang out with other couples.

2. **Loss of safety and decreased security:** My father-in-law was a doctor, who practiced for over forty years. As a result, we never ever needed to consult a general physician. He passed away in 2023, after which I remember falling ill and suddenly, felt like there was no one to call. It felt like a loss of comfort and decreased security. For years, we could always depend on him; suddenly realizing that he was not there meant that we needed to reimagine what safety meant all over again when it came to sickness and physical health.

   Safety can be seen from different perspectives; for example, some women in therapy after their partner's loss talk about how lost and unsafe they feel as their partner took care of their needs in every way, including finances. For young adult children, who lose a parent very early to death, their sense of stability is shaken. Saira, a fourteen-year-old in a therapy session, told me, 'My parents travel quite a bit and the only constant person around was my grandma. Now that she is no more, I feel alone and scared. I don't know what to do. I can't explain this to my friends as I feel guilty telling them that I'm not close to my parents.'
3. **Loss of hope and meaning-making:** Our loved one's presence gives us a reason to live and hope. When we lose a loved one, we feel that all that anchored us, kept us going and brought a sense of purpose to us has been taken away. Ramona told me, 'My elder sister was like a parent to me. She was my cheerleader and always optimistic. Making my sister happy and proud was my life's goal. When she passed away, I felt I had no desire to live. My ambition began to dwindle and I suddenly felt life was so meaningless.'

When people lose loved ones to suicide, homicide, unfortunate circumstances or chronic health conditions, very often people feel all that they believed in and had faith in has been impacted and shaken to the very core. A sentiment that keeps showing up in therapy is about people consistently asking, 'Why me?'. They don't know what they can hold on to as an anchor or belief system. These are moments where grieving individuals feel conflicted and can't make sense of why their loved one, who was so giving and loving, had to die. Milind, who lost his neighbour during the pandemic, asked me in a session, 'I always thought if you lead a good life, good will happen to you. Now I wonder why bad things happen to good people. All that felt hopeful and gave me meaning just slipped away, when my young friend Sumesh passed away. I feel distraught and hopeless.'

Activity

Secondary Loss Checklist

Tick the ones you have experienced in the aftermath of grief.

Sense of Safety

Financial challenges
Lifestyle changes
Loss of income
Loss of security
Moving of houses and the idea of home getting impacted
Loss of familiarity and comfort

Interpersonal Relationships

Distance in friendships
Loss of friendships
Betrayal/abandonment experienced with family, friends, or siblings

One's Sense of Self and World View

Loss of hope
Lack of purpose and meaning-making
Decreased motivation
Loss of shared memories
Decreased confidence
Loss of faith
Loss of autonomy and ability to make choices
Loss of innocence
Loss of companionship/possible future

The list I have provided is not exhaustive and I'm aware that there are many I would have missed out. As you read this, consider making your own list of personal secondary losses.

Dealing with Secondary Losses

1. **Permission to feel:** One of the reasons that grief feels overwhelming is because there is so much to deal with. Sometimes, we don't even make space for our secondary losses. When my father-in law passed away, I realized that I was suppressing and not even acknowledging these losses.

   My therapist friend gently nudged me to make a list of all that seems to be impacting me. While making the list itself seemed daunting, it helped me in acknowledging and giving myself the permission to feel the secondary losses. Whether it's journalling with specific prompts, morning pages or free-flow writing, all of them are some ways we can choose to express our grief, irrespective of what our grieving style may be.
2. **Pause:** As we acknowledge the secondary losses, it's important to pause and recognize that all of them don't need to be addressed right away. Learning to step back and sit with our feelings in relation to the secondary losses is crucial, too. As we do the work of processing our grief, how we respond to these secondary losses also changes. Rita, after her husband's loss, felt a deep sense of insecurity as she didn't know how to handle financial matters. As she began talking about it to her close friends and son, they volunteered to help her and suggested that since finances weren't an immediate concern, she address them a month later. This helped, as in the first few days of loss, she was very fragile.

   I tell clients to remember that the helplessness and strong intensity we attach to secondary losses also shifts as we do the grief work. So, learning to not underplay our losses but hold them gently is crucial. We need to remember that our intense feelings about situations and people can be fleeting, too, so this is not the time to make absolute judgments or take impulsive stands. It helps to buy time before we respond. If you are in therapy, talk about your secondary losses and the feelings that accompany them.

3. **Choose whether you want to engage or not:** When it comes to loss of friendships or absences in relationships in the light of grief, stay with what is happening but be mindful of not becoming disillusioned just yet. Very often, clients tell me that they experience an urge to tell others about their absence or send a message when in the midst of intense emotion. A good idea is to give yourself permission to feel anger and rage. At the same time, pause and ask yourself if you really want to engage and how it will help in this moment of grief. A client mentioned how she sent a message on a weekend to a close family member about their not showing up. She never got a reply, although it was read. The client told me how it infuriated her further and made her feel more hurt.

   In the age of technology, I tell clients to try and not rage-text when they are hurting. If you need to host a conversation with a friend or relative and feel that it's important for you, tell them that you missed their presence and wondered why they didn't show up. A good idea is to have these conversations in person and if they are away, maybe on a virtual phone call, but not via messages or chat. My sense is that we need to be realistic about the fact that the person we are sharing our disappointment and hurt with may have a blind spot or may not have the capacity to understand what we are saying. We need to remember that even if the other person chooses to apologize, sometimes the grieving individual may continue feeling hurt or find the apology insincere. So, giving yourself time before you open up dialogue is crucial.

Lean in: What helps the most when it comes to dealing with these losses is to identify folks who have been present, understand your reality and are ready to listen. Identify the ways in which you need support; if it helps, join a support group that allows you to talk about the losses and find a community.

As we begin to do the work of rebuilding our life and grief integration, we slowly learn to work through our secondary losses and even reimagine relationships differently.

29

Mixed Feelings

'I miss my mum and can't stop crying. At the same time, I still feel rage and sadness thinking that she never accepted me and my partner.'

'I hated what drugs did to my son and felt angry at him. But I feel so much love for him too, and he is no longer here, so I don't know what to do with all the love I have. I'm broken.'

These are sentences spoken by clients in therapy sessions, depicting ambivalent feelings they experience about their loved one, who is no more.

Relational ambivalence is a part of our life. When it comes to our parents, partners, children and our friends, we do find ourselves in situations where we experience ambivalence. A good way to understand the term 'ambivalence' is to look at it as a state where the individual experiences mixed feelings; in most instances, it is strong opposing feelings. Grief is complex and when there are mixed feelings towards the person who passed away or the relationship you shared with them, it gets harder.

One example of ambivalence is when you experience deep love for the person and at the same time, are consumed by a feeling of shame because of their actions. You may feel and know that a parent loves you, yet in their actions and words, it seems otherwise; you feel confusion and don't feel seen or heard by them. Yet, in a society where there is so much pressure to never utter a negative word about the person who has passed away, when people experience ambivalent feelings in relation to grief, it takes a while before they can openly share it. Even when they do, grieving individuals experience guilt and shame for bringing up these so called 'negative feelings'.

Mohini, a fifty-year-old client, who I have known and seen in therapy for five years, told me, 'I'm kind of relieved that my husband is no more. You know I didn't hate him, but in the last few years, his dependence on drugs and then alcohol left me feel unloved, exhausted and hypervigilant. Whenever the phone rang, I would think that he had gotten into an accident due to drunk driving. I was tired of being put in awkward situations, feeling a sense of shame. At the same time, I can't stop thinking about him and how much he loved me. He knew me like no one else, he was a good man and a good father. I'm stuck in a place where I can breathe a bit easy, but now that he is not there, I wonder what's the point of living.'

Mohini felt relief that her husband was finally gone, and she no longer needed to worry about being ashamed. At the same time, she burst out crying and said that she was an evil person because she was only thinking about herself. Our ambivalence evokes a feeling of cognitive dissonance, a discomfort and tension emanating from the push and pull that we experience. Grief makes it hard for us to make sense of what's emerging in us, and ambivalent feelings make it harder. They can leave us feeling confused and distraught with pain about the loss alongside anger towards our own self for having mixed feelings.

While ambivalence is felt very commonly, it remains a topic that's not much discussed, even in the therapy fraternity. As a result, sometimes therapists themselves may not be aware of how to work or address it, when it does make an appearance.

What I have learnt from working with clients is that grief often gets prolonged, and integration gets tougher, particularly if there is an ambivalent relationship. As a result, this can come in the way of acceptance of loss and the meaning-making process.

Here are certain scenarios where ambivalence is more likely to show up.

Secrets That Unfold in the Aftermath of Grief

There are times when secrets begin to unfold in the aftermath of grief and they not only take the form of secondary loss, but also trauma. Most of these secrets can show up in the form of infidelity, debt, financial scandals, bankruptcy, legal matters and then information about the deceased having a second family.

Rajiv, a twenty-year-old male in therapy, mentioned, 'I was going through my dad's phone for bank documents and found pictures and videos that seemed very inappropriate, suggesting that he was seeing a family friend's wife for some years. I chanced upon this evidence and ended up throwing up for the entire day. I don't know what to do with it, and if I should tell my mum about it. I'm angry, sad and broken from within. I hate him for what seems like an affair and at the same time, I love him and miss him so much. He was my role model. My heart hurts, and I can't tell anyone about this.'

As secrets unfold, they can leave family members or the person in the family who found out or stumbled upon them in a state of shock, disbelief and betrayal. In those moments, when these secrets are discovered, the grief begins to shift and suddenly, ambivalence creeps in. Like Rajiv, who was disgusted by those messages and what his dad had done but couldn't stop missing him either.

Neglect, Absence of Love, Trauma, Humiliation and Unresolved Lingering Feelings

For clients who have been in family set-ups where there is a conflictual relationship with a parent, sibling or loved one—either due to violence, a history of trauma, neglect, physical abuse, emotional abuse, alcoholism, addiction and so on—it leads to mixed feelings. Particularly when it comes to addiction of any kind, family members find themselves in a hard space. They talk about how hard it is for them to have empathy for the person struggling with addiction and at the same time, the love that they feel and receive keeps them in the relationship.

Estrangement, Abandonment and Loss of Contact Before Death

People who have been at the receiving end of estrangement or felt abandoned by their families are more likely to experience ambivalence. It is heightened when for years, you lost contact with a loved one or chose to not speak to them, or if they chose to cut ties with you.

Naomi, a client who underwent a gender reassignment surgery, told me how her parents cut all ties with her when she came out and decided to go ahead with it. She mentioned how her father would still wish her, but her mum never saw her, wished her or even checked about her well-being. When her mum passed away, she told me, 'I don't know what to do. I'm going to the funeral, but I don't know if my mum would have wanted it. I feel seething anger towards my mum but the memory of her holding my hand when I was a child, gently stroking my hair when I couldn't sleep and always supporting my dream of being a writer evoke so much love for her and I miss her.'

The reality is that these mixed feelings may have existed for very long, but a loss means that we have to address them now and there is no running away.

Estrangement experienced in relation to siblings, and immediate family can evoke feelings of abandonment. I have worked with clients where their parent or a primary caregiver left home and disappeared, never to be found. In all those set-ups, family members were left with questions and ambivalent feelings that can be difficult to make sense of.

Long-Standing Caregiving, Defiance and Mental Health Conditions

In set-ups where you have been caregiving for a family member who's defiant, not supportive or accepting of treatment, sometimes towards the end, the caregiver may begin to experience ambivalent feelings. This is also true for set-ups where the caregiver has been present for someone who's struggling with a long-standing illness.

In therapy, I have also seen that clients begin to struggle with mixed opposing feelings as they see their loved ones go through illnesses such as schizophrenia and dementia.

Kareena told me, 'My granddad was my favourite person in the world. He is the one who always made me feel seen, appreciated and said that I was the best thing that happened to the world. I made a choice to not go abroad because he was in India. When he was 82 years old, he started becoming paranoid, impulsive, forgetting things and using language he had never used before. Then, when doctors diagnosed him with dementia, we could make sense of what was happening. At the same time, all these symptoms evoked all sorts of feelings, including sadness, rage and helplessness. Now that he is no more, I feel guilty for getting angry at him. I don't know how to make sense of all my feelings.'

Death by Suicide

Death by suicide evokes a feeling of shock, betrayal and disbelief. Knowing that a family member, whom you loved, ended their life can evoke ambivalence at all levels. In most situations, when clients reach out in therapy because a loved one died by suicide, they are distraught, but most importantly each one of them feels abandoned and wonder if their love was not enough for the deceased to share their suffering. They also deeply know that the person who passed away really cared for them and possibly took the step as they were really struggling. Yet, making sense of all these feelings, coming to terms with them and emotionally acknowledging them is hard and it evokes ambivalence, which is hard even to talk about.

Activity

If you have experienced ambivalent feelings when it comes to grief due to either of these scenarios or something that I missed mentioning, take a few moments to write down what's emerging for you. A good idea is to let the thoughts and feelings flow as you put them down on paper. At the same time, if reading this chapter has been overwhelming and is proving to be a trigger, I would suggest that you take a break from reading and come back to this at a later time.

____

____

____

____

____

____

____

How to Deal with Ambivalence

Ambivalence is a normal part of grieving. Ambivalence is not easy to share at all, especially in families where it is believed that 'all family matters should remain within the four walls of the house'. Where the parent or other siblings choose to never address ambivalence, it gets harder for people to give themselves permission to articulate the mixed feelings. However, what we know is ambivalence in grief, if not addressed, can come in the way of grief integration. It can leave the person feeling a consistent agitation and anxiety as opposing feelings continue to linger.

Sigmund Freud, in his work titled. *Mourning and Melancholia*, talks about ambivalence. He mentions that if there was a high degree of ambivalence between the deceased and the grieving individual in the context of their relationship, it can come in the way of the mourning process and possibly lead to melancholia.

My experience in situations where ambivalence is not addressed with close friends or family is that it can take various forms—sometimes it becomes shame or hatred towards one's own self, and at other times a sense of disillusionment and avoidance when it comes to relationships.

Here is how you can begin to work through ambivalence:

1. Begin by acknowledging that it's alright and normal to experience mixed feelings and ambivalence.
2. Make space for recognizing that mixed feelings that are opposing and contradictory can be experienced

simultaneously. This can be hard, and while our mind would want to wish them away and not deal with them, one needs to learn to sit with difficult feelings.

3. Choose to be self-compassionate and hold space for yourself, even if you don't understand where these feelings are coming from and the reasons that underlie the feelings.
4. Very often, clients feel that they are being petty or trivial when they feel these emotions. Choose to not judge yourself for what you are feeling. It's a good idea to see feelings as pleasant or unpleasant sensations, rather than look at them as positive or negative feelings.
5. Make space for patience: As we do the hard work of acknowledging ambivalence, we need to remember that it's not easy. Learning to not rush ourselves and get done with it is important. In fact, during the early days of loss, I tell clients to not be hasty in trying to find a solution for all that is emerging. We need to be mindful that being patient with ourselves is an action step. Given that loss takes our basic sense of control away from us, this act of patience can feel like you are being passive and not really proactively doing anything about the overwhelming pain that you are feeling.

As Dr Alexandra Solomon, a well-known author and psychotherapist mentioned in one conference, 'The opposite of ambivalence isn't certainty, it's patience.' It's a way of being present for ourselves and letting things be.

Holding the ambivalence: Esther Perel and Mary Alice Walker mention in a column, 'We often think we need to resolve the tension and come to a resolution. Sometimes we do (in abusive relationships, especially). In most situations, however, holding the ambivalence is in itself a form of radical acceptance. This may be true for how we accept our relationships and for how we accept ourselves.'[1]

My experience has been that even in the context of grief, the act of holding two opposing feelings and accepting this duality is healing in itself.

Psychotherapy

When there are mixed feelings that seem to be intense, frequent and at the same time evoke a sense of guilt, shame or blame within us, the process of psychotherapy can help. It can help people to articulate their mixed feelings and express it as they experience it. Like Monit, who lost his brother to suicide, shared, 'After my brother's death, I keep seeing my him in my dreams. He's never sad or unhappy, just present. But I can't make sense of my own feelings, where on one day I blame myself for his death, which I know is not true, and on the other day, I blame him for being selfish. This also I know is not true, as he must have really suffered to take such a big step. It's been a year, and I haven't managed to say this out loud to anyone. It feels lighter now that I'm able to say it for the first time.'

Therapy can become a psychological safe space, where clients can choose to work through ambivalence and learn that they won't be judged or blamed for it. When clients begin to do the work, and have the capacity to hold two opposing emotions, I encourage them to focus on how they have dealt with ambivalence in the past.

A huge part of accepting ambivalence and a step towards integration is acknowledging that we are capable of loving people and yet stay aware of our own unmet needs in relation to them. It also means recognizing that people we loved had their own struggles, which we don't completely understand or ever will.

The final task of accepting ambivalence is knowing that we can live with it, and we don't need to continually look for closure or a reason.

30

Closure

Questions about closure are something that I'm asked over and over again in therapy sessions, in various forms. Questions such as, 'What do you think closure looks like?', or 'Do I need to reach closure, for the process of healing to be complete?', and 'What if I don't believe in closure?', often come up.

Clients enter therapy in the light of a divorce, a terrible break up, abandonment and then grief to find answers, and sometimes with the hope that the therapy process will offer closure. They believe that therapy can help them with some resolution, possibly an answer.

My understanding is that our fundamental attitude when it comes to looking at grief is flawed, whereby we believe that people will deal with the loss, recover and move on. The idea of closure and the importance it assumes comes from there. As a result, whether it is our colleagues, well-meaning friends or family members, many with the intention of supporting us ask repeatedly if we have found closure. To them, finding closure means we are doing well and recovering. As we discussed in the last section, watching other people's grief and seeing them grieve can be discomforting and sometimes, I wonder if others hoping that the grieving individual reaches a stage of closure has something to do with it.

The term 'closure' can be quite misleading. It assumes a certain finality, which is not what we can have in relation to loss and grief. The term closure at its core means 'tying up all the ends' for some people. The Merriam Webster Dictionary provides various definitions for the term and one of them is 'an often comforting or satisfying sense of finality'. It also defines it as 'an act of closing'.

The idea that closure is necessary for people to process and integrate their grief can come in the way of their grieving and healing process.

Our healing can happen without a sense of closure.

I don't think we can reach a stage of closure when it comes to loss. Losing a loved one doesn't mean that we stop loving them. Our love continues for them, and we find a new way for the bond to continue. As Pauline Boss, who's a family therapist, says in her book, *The Myth of Closure: Ambiguous Loss in a Time of Pandemic and Change*, 'Continuing to use the term "closure" perpetuates the myth that losses and grief have a prescribed time for ending—or never starting—and that it's emotionally healthier to close the door on suffering than to face it and learn to live with it.'[1] In her work, she talks about how the illusory idea about closure can often make us stray.

As a result, when clients ask about closure, I ask them to define what closure means for them. My sense is that finding closure is an internal and subjective process and, as a result, it looks different for everyone. For some people, closure feels like acceptance, making peace with the fact that their loved one is no more; for others, it's acceptance that when their loved one passed away, it was time for them to go.

Sometimes, closure is learning to accept that there aren't any answers out there. Even if we go over the reports again and again or replay scenarios in our head, realizing that there is no sense of certainty or singular answers in death is closure. For others, learning to surrender and accepting the loss is what closure looks like. Then there are others, for whom meaning-making and building new hope can feel like closure.

It is okay for us to not find closure or even look for it. Love never really goes away, so how can there be closure?

Our very identity and presence become a continuation of the person we loved and the impact they had on us. Aren't our lives so much about the people we loved and how they shaped us? And if that's the truth, then we will be fine even in the absence of closure?

As human beings, we can live our life again, fostering hope and yet hold the loss, and carry the love in our heart for our loved one.

Dealing with loss becomes a masterclass in ambiguity, where you know that the pieces will never be found to the puzzle and yet, you will eventually find a way to make sense of what life has to offer.

31

Dreams

Does everyone dream of their loved one, who has passed away?

Do these dreams continue to change as one does the work in therapy?

Grief dreams or bereavement dreams are common in the aftermath of loss. At the same time, not everyone who is grieving has these dreams. **It's completely okay if you have not seen a loved one who passed away ever in your dreams, or if you don't remember dreams at all. Choose to not judge yourself over it.**

An article published by the Pew Research Centre, written by Patricia Tevington and Manolo Corichi, talks about how 53 per cent of adults in the US said that they had been visited by a dead family member in a dream or some other form. It was found that women, more than men, reported having these interactions with dead family members. The research also stated that 'people who are moderately religious are more likely than others—including those who are highly religious and those who are *not* religious—to have experienced these things.'[1]

In my experience, for some grieving individuals, such dreams can be extremely calming and soothing. For others, the dreams can come across as disturbing and nightmarish; there are also others, who can't figure out what it means or signifies. I have worked with clients who, in the aftermath of loss, have dreams where everything literally seems to be falling apart, and then have dreams that don't seem to make sense to them, but end in death or injury. There are also those who continually see dreams that depict helplessness, inevitability, inconsolably crying and feelings of abandonment. These dreams can come in the way of sleep and in case of traumatic grief, often there are nightmares that are deeply unsettling.

Some of my clients have also talked about how their loved one came in their dream to give them a message, which helped them with meaning-making. When this happens, they feel that they found their sense of closure through their dreams. There are instances where clients have reported that a loved one made it to their dream to tell them that they are in a good place or at other times, to tell them that they couldn't have done anything better or differently. These dreams can help clients in a big way and are very crucial to the journey of grief integration. There are also dreams where we feel the love or the loving gaze with which the person who passed away is looking at us or telling us something, and those dreams can feel like an anchor, comforting and soothing, a reminder yet again that love continues.

For clients struggling and dealing with ambivalent feelings towards their loved one, very often dreams become a window to these mixed feelings, even if they are not aware of them. Slow and gentle work using dreams and what it symbolically means can help in a big way to address what is being evoked in the client and for them to make meaning and accept their loss.

Sometimes, as people continue to do the work, not only do the dreams change, but the feelings that are experienced in these dreams also change. Peter was forty-one when he came to therapy as he felt that he was struggling with depression and his capacity to engage with people was declining. He had been successful and was always perceived as extremely reliable and happy-go-lucky, so it was a shock for his family that he thought he needed therapy. As we did the work, we talked about any trauma experiences that he may have had. He talked about his mum's death due to cancer. He had lost his mum when he was eleven and for years after that, he would have dreams about his mother leaving them and going away somewhere far. In the dreams, Peter would feel that even if he tried, he couldn't stop her. As a result, he would end up feeling a sense of abandonment. He was always close to his mother, and he knew that she always had loved him, so these dreams didn't make any sense to him. The ambivalence in the dreams was the reason that he had never shared this with anybody, not even his own father.

After the loss, the family didn't really speak about the loss and how each one was feeling. They started moving on and rebuilding their lives. Years later, he started telling me about his dreams and how each of them had a thread of abandonment. As we did the grief work, which was not easy, and slowly worked through what Peter was experiencing, it became apparent that there was delayed grief that had never been addressed. As Peter came to see this, the dreams began to change, and he no longer felt abandoned or angry. He began to understand that the silence the family observed after the grief was a pattern that existed, and maybe his father didn't know any better. The theme of abandonment began to dissolve, and he could see his mum as a warm presence and being part of their life. He told me in one session, 'I seem to be more at peace. I miss her but, in the dream, she is always smiling and so are we. They are calming dreams, almost as if she is visiting me.'

Grief dreams are very common. At the same time, grieving individuals often don't talk about this as they feel others may judge them for having dreams or misinterpret their dreams. My experience is that dreams offer a rich source of information about how people are processing their grief, their beliefs and a window into leftover feelings that clients may not be able to articulate. So, making space for it in conversations can help people in their personal grief journey.

Part 5

Together We Will Be Alright

32

What Do We Want to Hear from Friends and Family?

> Deep grief sometimes is almost like a specific location, a coordinate on a map of time. When you are standing in that forest of sorrow, you cannot imagine that you could ever find your way to a better place. But if someone can assure you that they themselves have stood in that same place, and now have moved on, sometimes this will bring hope.
>
> —Elizabeth Gilbert

Elizabeth Gilbert's quote is a reminder of how others' journeys can help us deal with our own grief, which may feel unique. And yet, when others provide witnessing and we see them responding to life, it gives us hope. When there is grief, it is not just the individual who is impacted, but the family, friendships, intimate relationships, our work and how we see the world. Given this understanding, learning to deal with grief requires an ecosystem of people who provide psychological and emotional safety for grieving individuals to address what's emerging in them.

When you encounter someone who has lost a loved one, this section will help you with what to say and, importantly, what not to say.

One of the things that I often hear clients and family tell me is that they don't know how to word a message or worry about saying the wrong things. This section is an attempt at offering some tips, choice of words and ideas about how to navigate these conversations.

1. **The gift of presence:** Presence is the biggest gift we can offer to someone when they are grieving. While it sounds simple, it provides a soothing balm. Show up for others and be present—it makes a huge difference. When I lost my father, although I had been prepared for years, what really helped was friends and family showing up. Their physical presence and being surrounded by others who understood the pain made it easier to go through the day. I realized that all the grief I was holding inside found its way out as I spoke more and more about it to those present and that we could share a hug. As Cori Doerrfeld says in the book, *The Rabbit Listened*, 'Sometimes, hugs say more than words.'

   Very often, people worry about saying the right thing, but what's most important is to be present. Even if you are listening or just there to support someone, your presence itself can help the person grieving feel supported and less alone, at a time where even making the simplest decision seems tough and everything seems to be overwhelming.
2. **Check in**: One of my friends, while leaving from the prayer meeting after my father's passing, said to me that she would text every day—and it really mattered. I don't think I would have been able to ask for it or even had the strength to call anyone. A simple check-in on the lines of, 'How are you feeling today?' or 'I'm thinking of you and here for you', can mean the world to the bereaved. Ask open-ended questions. At the same time,

remember that the bereaved may take time to respond and may not be able to articulate what they are feeling. We are more likely to remember and appreciate friends, family members and colleagues who showed up and did a check-in, versus those who just didn't check on our well-being.

The harder part of processing and dealing with the grief begins once the rituals are done. That's when people need the most support and often, clients in therapy tell me, 'Once the rituals are done, it's as if people stop coming or checking in. A part of me felt massively lonely and alone in my grief.' So, a check-in and being present beyond the rituals and ceremonies creates space for the grief to be seen and understood.

3. **Make a choice to be available:** Very often, when people are grieving, they may not be able to ask for support. Choose to be around to help with practical chores, such as preparing for the funeral, a ritual or when the cupboard that belonged to the person who passed away is being cleared. Taking responsibility for things, such as seeing to it that your grieving friend or relative eats and their children are taken care of, can be helpful. Clients have shared how, when friends and family offer to pack children's school lunches, volunteer to pick and drop the kids home or say they will come and help with the house and meals, it really helps. So, when friends and family say, 'I'm a call away', you appreciate that.

I read this beautiful blog by Hugh Hollowell, titled 'Grief Groceries', which is a reminder of what help can look like. In his blog, Hugh shares a story about how when his dad passed away, a friend who had met his dad only once texted him, asking, 'Will you be home at 8.30 p.m. tonight?' This friend lived twelve hours away from Hugh. When Hugh responded saying yes, she texted him, saying, 'Instacart will be there at 8.30 p.m., open the door for them.' At 8.30 p.m., when he opened the door, he realized that she had sent two boxes full of groceries. As Hugh says, describing the box in the blog, '[There were] Things I could heat up if I needed a meal, or pig out on if I needed fat and sugar. Sometimes, you just need to eat half a box of Oreos.'[1]

This is a beautiful reminder of how thoughtful gestures can feel so helpful in our moments of grief. The reality is that when we are grieving, we are in a haze, and it is hard to be aware of what we need or what help would benefit us. A friend, who knows that I love watching plays, a month after my dad's loss said, 'I know you haven't gone out much, let me know if you are free on Sunday, I can book tickets for a play you would love.' I agreed and went for it. Sometimes, presence—along with kind and mindful gestures—can feel like a warm hug.

4. **Ask mindful questions that hold space for the person dealing with their loss:** Grief never feels the same and each day brings its own rollercoaster of emotions. I remember when my father-in law passed away, a friend asked, 'Were you close to him?' These questions, when asked sensitively with the intention of listening, can evoke a lot. As a grieving person, each of these questions also becomes a way of processing and making sense of what has happened.

   Questions or statements that reflect the intensity of loss and the pain that the person who is bereaved is experiencing allow for a conversation to unfold.
5. **Get comfortable with silence:** Ramesh, a fifty-five-year-old male client, told his family after he lost his brother that he loved having family friends over at home, but felt that he was not ready to talk about his

feelings yet. He told them that at this stage, 'All I want is presence, affection and hugs.' In a session, he mentioned that a few friends and a close cousin visited him on many evenings and would have tea with him—a ritual he had shared with his brother for years. But Ramesh and his friends would not talk much. They would either listen to songs, watch the sunset or do something else. Gradually, he started heading out for walks; eventually, his grief found words.

His friends and family respected his needs, which is very crucial when one is offering support to an individual who's grieving.

6. **Make room for patience:** Grief is messy and can look different to each person. For all the clients I have worked with, there are similar threads and patterns that underlie the grieving process, but it is never the same. As we discussed in an earlier chapter, grief has no timelines. So, learning to be patient means avoiding statements that either trivialize their grief or make them feel that you want them to get done with it. Saumya told me, 'A friend keeps asking me, "So what's new?" I hate that question. My friend knows that it's been less than a week since my partner's death and all I do is look at his pictures. There are days I just want to block her and not receive her call. I love her as a friend and she was amongst the first few people who showed up, but I almost feel that she wants me to quickly get over this and move on.'

   My understanding is that it takes a village to help us to deal with our grief. Support in every form counts. Micro-interactions in which others provide attentive presence and witnessing to our grief give us strength and hope.

Some of the things that friends and family said and did, which I found useful in my moment of loss, were:

- A friend sent me a copy of the book, *The Rabbit Listened*, and said, 'I'm your rabbit. Always around.'
- A neighbour brought dinner and said, 'I can drop it and leave if you don't feel like talking'.
- My daughter's friend's mother said, 'The children have exams going on. If you want, I can come to pick her up and drop her off to school, and she can also stay with us. I can bring her back home whenever you wish.'
- I was not heading out much; a friend asked me when I was free and said he would plan for us to hang out and go to an art exhibition I had been meaning to see.
- Family, colleagues who showed up, listened and validated what I was feeling.
- A friend said, 'You have a lot to deal with and do. Let me help you work through this. I will come to your house, and we can figure it out together.'
- A close friend said, 'I'm coming right away so that I'm there for the cremation and prayer meet.'
- At the cremation, friends decided to sort out the paperwork that needed to be done for a death certificate.
- Relatives and neighbours arranged for the food for the first few days.
- A friend who just sat with me and held my hand. She said, 'We don't need to talk if you don't want. I'm here for you.'
- Friends, relatives and acquaintances, who shared their vulnerable moments, their grief and said that it is hard. The honesty and vulnerability and knowing that others have gone through loss and slowly dealt with it helped.
- Everyone who continued to check in gently, beyond the rituals and the first month.

33

What Doesn't Work and What Not to Say

Sometimes, what's worse than the silence is the comments and advice given that nullify or diminish people's pain and suffering. Very often, a lot that is said is unintentional and coming from a good place, or an extension of people's value system. At the same time, for a grieving person, it can come across as either insensitive or unkind, and can even make them feel that their grief is not being seen or understood by others.

1. **Don't burden people with responsibilities:** Koel, after losing her father, told me, 'I'm angry today. One of our relatives, who came to visit us, kept mentioning how I now needed to take charge and take care of my mum. Now that my dad was not there, all the responsibilities were mine. I know all this and I'm going to take care of my mum. But when it's been only two days since he passed away, I feel I have a right to grieve and miss him. Being reminded of what all lies ahead feels like a burden. The timing of that conversation felt like I didn't have a right to take care of my grief.' Some people unintentionally give advice which can come across as hurtful, insensitive and unhelpful.
2. **Don't tell them what they should be feeling:** There are different ways that the expression of grief can take. There

is no right or wrong way to grieve. Passing judgments or implying what people should or should not be feeling is unhelpful. It strips away their basic right to grieve and implies that there is only one way to do so. Some people can feel numb for months, others may have a delayed reaction; there are those who spend specific periods in denial or feeling angry. The only way we can really support someone is by respecting their personal journey around grief.

3. **Don't impose meaning-making:** Our sense of closure and making peace when a loved one passes away is a function of the relationship we shared with them, and the inner work we do. Very often, in the pursuit of helping others, people end up offering theories, whereby they try and supply perspectives in the hope that the grieving person may find it easier to deal with the loss. A client told me, 'I don't believe in God and when people try and explain my cousin's death using religious principles, I get very irritated. An aunt sent me a couple of links so that I could read and find my closure. I'm okay with what others do, but I have very little tolerance when people bombard me with religious and spiritual literature.' It's important to remember that it's okay if people don't find closure. It's also alright if it takes months or years for people to find closure and meaning-making.
4. **Don't say that time will heal:** The reality with grief is that we never really recover from it. It's not an illness that one finds a cure and treatment plan for. Whether it is loss due to death, separation or abandonment, there is a void left behind. Grief stays, and when people do the inner work, grief changes and looks different. However, there are no timelines to this process. So, telling people that it will get easier with passing time doesn't work. It can often make the grieving person feel that you are diminishing or trivializing their loss.

As people learn to make meaning of their grief and work towards accepting and acknowledging the loss, they begin to make peace with it. The charge attached to the grief begins to reduce. Yet, for everyone who has dealt with loss, we all know that grief comes in waves. Years after losing a loved one, a song that one hears and reminds us of our loved one could get us emotional and, in those moments, it can feel like grief never really left us.

5. **Don't say 'get over it':** Most of us have heard this in some way or the other, haven't we? Whether it's friends or family with the best intentions, sometimes they tell us to move on. How can one get over the immense love one has felt and the longing that continues? We need to acknowledge that there is no getting over grief.

   We learn to live with the loss and memories and build a life around it—that's the best we can do.

6. **Don't tell people to think about the road ahead:** Very often, relatives and friends with the best intentions tell the bereaved to 'think ahead and about their future'. While this advice comes from a place where they may want the bereaved to deal with their grief, it can come across as being insensitive and premature. For a person who has lost a loved one, their world has come to a standstill. Thinking about the future or making plans for it seems meaningless and impossible for a while. Abeer, a twenty-seven-year-old, who lost his wife to a car accident, told me, 'My brother, two months after my wife's death, asked me to start thinking about my future, about marriage and falling in love again. I know he cares for me, but I would have really appreciated it if he had asked how I am coping and what I miss, rather than being so obsessed with my future. I struggle to sleep and my tears don't stop when I listen to certain songs or eat my wife's favourite meal. I'm not ready to move on and think about the future.'

We need to recognize that for a person who's grieving, looking at the future may not be a solution when the loss still feels raw and fresh. What they need most at that point is people around them who understand the complex emotions they are experiencing all at once, and the sorrow they are left with. Everyone will eventually find their own path that helps them move towards the future. Though at a time when one is in the throes of grief, pressure and consistent rushing can come in the way of healing for the individual who is trying to make sense of a world without their loved one.

As Abeer shared 'My wife *was* my future, she was the reason I looked forward to every holiday, every day. Now, when the world tells me that I should look ahead, I have no answers. They don't understand me and my loss. I don't have the energy anymore.'

7. **Don't say, 'I know exactly what it feels like'**: Very often, when someone has experienced a similar loss, such as the loss of a parent or a partner, they may overshare and think that you will experience the pain like they did, and so, will also recover in the same way. I remember Romi, a client who I had worked with for many years, told me in a session after his mum's loss, 'My friend keeps comparing his grief journey to mine. He lost his mum a year ago and they weren't very close and shared a complex relationship. I felt deeply connected to my mum, spoke to her every day and now, I feel completely lost and unanchored. I really wish people would stop comparing and saying things like, "I know exactly how you feel," because nobody really knows.'

   If you are supporting someone who is dealing with grief, avoid these statements and instead, offer an attentive presence; learn to offer help in ways that feels helpful to the grieving person.

As an act of extending empathy and presence to others, particularly if you have experienced grief which is like theirs, remember what Brené Brown says in her book, *Atlas of The Heart*, 'We need to dispel the myth that empathy is "walking in someone else's shoes". Rather than walking in your shoes, I need to learn how to listen to the story you tell about what it's like in your shoes and believe you even when it doesn't match my experiences.'[1]

Statements that don't come across as helpful in moments of grief:

- When people tried to tell me that I'm 'resilient' and will manage.
- Telling me I will get better (I didn't know if better what is I wanted).
- Telling me that I can't be crying so much six months into the loss, when I know he had a peaceful death.
- Asking me to call them if I needed anything (while this comes from a place of good intention, most people at the time of grief don't call others and sometimes, don't even know what to say or ask for; grief is very disorienting).
- When people kept saying that the hardest phase is over, and it will only get easier.
- Telling me that I should be strong now as everything depends on me.
- Spouting cliches like 'time is a big healer', 'this too shall pass' and 's/he lived a full life'.

34

Recognizing When We Need to Lean In

In 2023, when I had back-to-back difficult months with health emergencies, grief, renovation and much more, I remember meeting friends who had not known much about this. When I narrated a few things, one of them asked, 'If there was so much happening and things were this hard, why didn't you reach out or tell any of us, we could have been there for you.'

At one level, this statement itself was deeply healing and yet, I recognized that when I'm in crisis, I withdraw and choose to go on as if nothing has happened. I operate from a stance of not burdening others. So, while I may make time to process my grief and go for my own therapy sessions, I fail to realize how much care and help I'm surrounded by. As a result, I don't let others carry my grief and struggle with asking for help; I'm almost surprised when others offer it.

I see the same sentiment with so many clients in therapy, who also mention how they don't want to burden others with their grief and pain. We forget that if we withdraw or go into our own shell, many around us with the best intentions may not know the intensity of our pain and have no clue about how our grieving is continuing. **As a grieving person, we need to hold space for ourselves, but also be holding the door open, so that others can support us.** Sometimes, without realizing, we shut the door so tight that others who want to be supportive can't enter or even be there for us.

Our trauma experiences, patterns of neglect and even the nature of the attachment patterns we had, impact whether we reach out to others in moments of loss or not. Sometimes, we learn that we must depend only on ourselves because we fear others may abandon us. At other times, it's the role modelling we have seen and the messaging our family has passed down consciously or unconsciously over the years.

A lot of times, we may be unconsciously carrying the belief that we need to deal with our grief alone. Babita, a thirty-three-year-old client, told me, 'I have seen so much abandonment in my life that when my sister passed away, I couldn't ask for help. My worry was that if I didn't get the help, I would feel abandoned all over again. Then, I would have to deal with the sorrow and abandonment as well. These fears stop me from telling others anything.'

Learning to recognize and address what comes in the way of us receiving and asking for help can help us at a time when grief feels overwhelming.

We often associate dealing and managing our own emotions as a sign of resilience. What I have learnt in my work and experiences is, in fact, that our resilience lies in recognizing what we can handle by ourselves, and in which areas we may benefit if we reached out for help. Asking for help and being vulnerable is never easy. It can feel unnerving, but it's a huge sign of strength and a reminder of resilience. Being mindful and recognizing our own irrational and unhelpful beliefs in moments when we need support is crucial.

35

Techniques that Help in Grief

Here are some techniques that I have used over the years to work through what has emerged for me and in relation to my clients. These are some ways we can allow ourselves the permission to grieve and let emotions find their way.

1. **Choosing to write and let it out (journalling):** When grieving individuals are struggling with experiencing emotion and getting in touch with what they are feeling, writing can help. Sometimes, as they begin to write and describe what's happening to them, they may find a release. The process of writing allows us to access old memories and very often, as we do that, we can feel an emotion trickling out or the heaviness finds a release. Before recommending journalling, I do ask clients about their relationship with writing and if they even want to do it. A good idea is to check and self-examine: do you find writing useful, or does it leave you feeling more overwhelmed? While journalling has been touted as a solution for all, my experience is that it doesn't work for everyone, so learning to not impose this on yourself is important. We sustain behaviours that sit well with us and that we find merit in.

For me, as a child, writing really helped. It allowed me to access my emotions when I was struggling and yet found it hard to feel. Early on, I realized that I tend to fall into the trap of intellectualizing and solving things. So, keeping a journal next to my nightstand has helped on days when pain feels unbearable. Over the years, I have learnt to be gentle, and not judge or edit my feelings when I'm writing. I have also developed a greater tolerance for what's emerging and just letting emotions flow.

So, whether you do morning pages, focused writing with prompts or just penning down your thoughts, remember that it must work for you.

It's okay if journalling doesn't work—you will figure out another soothing mechanism, like crocheting, running or something else that allows you to find healing. Some of my clients have talked about how they record what they are feeling, a way of letting out, and then delete the message that they had sent to themselves. It helps them feel lighter.

2. **Maintaining a mood log:** 'Each day feels the same and sometimes, it worsens. Is there a way to track and recognize what's happening?' This is not an unusual statement to hear.

   Sometimes, if clients have the energy and willingness, I suggest that they maintain a log of their feelings and thoughts. For some clients, it gives them a sense of how each day and month looks so different.Very often, clients are in a state of so much pain and sorrow that they may not want to or even have the energy to do this. But when Sujit was struggling with grief and I had suggested that he maintain a log so that we can better understand what time of the day his moods oscillate the most, and he did so. Ten days later, when Sujit came for the session, he told me,' I realized evenings is when I'm succumbing to grief and my body almost tells me to drown all my worries in alcohol. I laugh about it on some days as I feel like I have become such a cliché.'

I suggested that it may be a good idea to go back to kickboxing in the evening, since he used to enjoy it, although over the years he had stopped those classes. The mood log helped with the realization and catching an unhelpful pattern that he was falling into. He thought about it and eventually went back to kickboxing, and it allowed him to deal with the overwhelming mood.

Two weeks later, he mentioned, 'If I'm out of my home, I realize that the desire to drink isn't as strong, and the workout has helped deal with the sharp feelings of grief. I have been able to avoid alcohol completely.'

Daily Log

	Thoughts	Feelings	Tasks I'm avoiding	Tasks I can get myself to engage in	What helped me cope better?
Morning					
Afternoon					
Evening					

Early on, when the grief is intense and overwhelming, maintaining a log definitely doesn't work. Learning when to introduce this into your routine is a decision that has to be carefully considered. Perhaps it may be good to seek the help of a therapist, who can work with you to make that decision based on their understanding of your inner world, and the intensity and frequency of pain. For some, looking back at the log helps, because on bad days they are able to track and see that there were good days, too. When we feel grief coming back intensely on certain days, we seem to forget our progress, so a log can feel like an anchor and a sign that we will eventually deal with this and have an easier day soon. It becomes a record of our inner landscape of emotions and also of our progress. **We become a witness to the ebb and flow of our own grief and begin to recognize how we are coping.**

3. **The body keeps the score:** Our body carries the grief, whether we remember the dates or don't. The body chooses to store the signs and even if cognitively, we don't remember it, the pain and sadness will show up. About seven years into my father's passing, I forgot that it was my father's death anniversary—but the day preceding it and, on that day, I felt this strange sadness consume me. The sorrow and its intensity seemed unexplainable. As I sat with the discomfort and allowed myself to do nothing, it dawned on me that it was my father's death anniversary. While I had forgotten the date, my body had remembered.

   As you read the book, I want you to become aware of what it's evoking in your body. We need to acknowledge that processing through grief requires not only grief integration, but also involves acknowledging and working through the pain that is stored in the body. **Just as the body keeps score of our longing and pain, it also keeps a record of the healing**. You will know when the body begins to heal and there is a lightness that can be experienced. So, paying attention to the body and the sensations one feels is the key. At the same time, learning not to be hypervigilant or over-focused is crucial.

4. **The role of physical exercise and movement:** Rishabh told me, 'When my wife died, I took to running. A friend said it helped him in his difficult time. Running became a time for me to cry, but also a reason to get out of our home, which I had struggled with for weeks. Before I took to running, I would obsessively look at my phone, scroll and just ruminate about what could be done. Running became a way of starting my day. Soon I was part of a running group and that meant new social connections and community—all of which I needed, that is people who were just around.'

   Research has shown that physical activity plays a crucial role when it comes to how we cope with grief. For me, long solitary walks have served as an anchor in moments of stress, anxiety and grief. I have felt that the grief fog begins to reduce, and I feel more in touch with my surroundings. The tightness and restlessness that's stuck in the body begins to ease up and I feel less mired in my own thoughts.

   Whether it's dance, swimming, t'ai chi, martial arts or strength training workouts, choose to engage in what soothes you. I remember Minoo, a client of mine, telling me, 'I have realized that with dance, all emotions that I suppress come to the surface. As the music plays, my tears roll, and it becomes a cathartic session. Without my dance class, I worry that I will bury myself under work and not give myself a chance to feel. So, two weeks into my husband's death, I joined the dance class, because I needed to stay in touch with what I was feeling. That's the way I honour my love for him.'

   My only advice to Minoo was to be mindful of the exhaustion she was experiencing and not overdo her dance lessons. A good idea is to always start gradually with any exercise; it is best to start with exercise one is used to and doesn't feel too intense.

5. **All those moments, where being out in nature saved me:** I remember a day after my father-in-law's funeral, when I stepped out to do some chores. On the street, as I was walking, I saw bright pink bougainvillea. That moment is etched in my head as it provided healing, a reminder of vitality and what it meant to be alive, which I had completely forgotten. Two days before that and till that moment, I was going through the motions and felt almost dead from within. This bright pink flower made me aware of how grief had taken over. In that moment, I felt one with nature. I felt as if I was taken out of my stupor and brought back to life. It was deeply healing. I used it as an anchor to keep reminding myself to come to the present as I dealt with the grief.

   I remember my therapist telling me to spend as much time as possible in nature after a loss. Being in nature is therapeutic. When we are grieving, our idea of what the world has to offer and what life means somehow seems to change. It seems like we are trapped; it is dark, lonely and there is no light. Being out in nature can feel like hope. The expansiveness and the sense of awe one experiences can be life-affirming. There is a certain rhythm and a place for the smallest of creatures in nature and sometimes, that kind of witnessing at a deeper level allows us to accept the way life is unfolding and still trust what is there to come.

   A good exercise would be for you to ask yourself how being out in nature provides your own healing and soothing.

6. **Saved by books, movies and shows:** For some of us whose emotions may go into hiding in moments of

crisis, recognizing what allows us to get in touch with our feelings is crucial. I find that listening to music allows me to feel and stay with what's emerging. Reading and watching shows is another way I sometimes process emotions as it offers a certain witnessing and relatability, which is what we need the most. At the same time, there are people who worry that they will fall into a pattern of binge-watching and, in turn, run away from their emotions. So, being aware of what watching and listening or even reading does for you is important.

There are some shows and movies that people can find extremely triggering when grief is raw, and one is experiencing acute loss. Learning to listen to what you are feeling is necessary. Clients have told me how watching Korean dramas has been deeply calming for them, like a gentle and warm hug. Then there are clients who have mentioned how shows such as *Fleabag, After Life, This Is Us, Ted Lasso* and *Shrinking* have helped them make sense of what they are going through and find relatability, humour and an acknowledgement of the paradox of life.

7. **Meditation:** The process of sitting with our grief and observing what's emerging in us is extremely helpful to some people in the light of grief. When it comes to sitting and honouring one's grief, a guided meditation, listening to soothing music that provides an ambience, is one way that people find a sense of grounding and anchoring. I have personally found solace in this. Early in grief, it would mean just sitting for a few minutes, and even these couple of minutes helped me to stay with the feelings that were emerging.

   Guided meditation has helped me find a sense of feeling centred even if it was for brief moments. At the same time, there are a lot of people who talk about how meditating can be very triggering for them, because their ruminative thoughts increase. For others, meditation sometimes brings back a flashback of a traumatic event and leaves them more anxious. Being mindful of what meditation evokes for you is important.

Meditation may not work for everyone and that's alright. That's why it's important to find what's helpful for you.

8. **Find what's self-soothing for you:** Choosing to identify and engage with what calms us is important. All acts of creation and tending to, such as gardening, crochet, drawing, painting and writing are life-affirming. They are reminders of hope and often, people feel that these processes hold them at a time when they don't even know what they want. Listening to calming music and playing an instrument is also a part of this. I have worked with clients who have described how witnessing art and creating art have worked for them. So, trusting yourself with what works for you is crucial.

   I have had clients, who have talked about how reading religious texts, going to a shrine and prayers have helped them find community and answers to questions they struggled with, or with closure. Over the years, clients and friends have talked about how their shift towards spirituality, reading certain texts, group classes on meditation and lectures that help them make sense of existential truths using various theosophical texts have all served as an anchor.

When it comes to dealing with grief, becoming mindful of techniques that can be helpful allows us to feel anchored in some way. These techniques often become a way of holding hope for our own self.

Epilogue

Of Grief and Love

I spent years anticipating the loss of my dad as he struggled with illness and hospitalization. The strange thing is that when he died in 2013, I recognized that I was so scared of his death that in all the years preceding it, I had become a ball of anxiety and fear. I found it hard to love deeply as I felt that this meant also accepting that the people I loved will be no more one day, and then grief will strike once again.

Even in his death, my father taught me how to live. It dawned upon me that how we accept and process grief impacts everything, I believe it shapes how we love and how we live.

This, in turn, also means that if we choose to suppress and avoid dealing with our grief, then in so many ways it starts coming in the way of how we love. I'm sure this lesson has always been around, spoken by philosophers, spiritual teachers and experienced by people who are grieving, but in my moment of loss it came alive, and over the years I gathered the courage to accept it. We all, in our own time, begin to acknowledge and accept this truth. It is a lesson that can save us and teach us how to embrace life, love and become more mindful in how we live.

We need to trust and believe that, as we deal with grief, there will be moments that will feel like healing. There is grace in acknowledging that as we grieve, and remembering that the love we shared and felt holds us together. What I have seen again and again in my office is how there is a strength and resilience that continues to shine as people deal with their grief. While we never really recover from grief, we find ways to live and love again. Trusting the process of grief and choosing to ask for help from friends, family and sometimes mental health professionals can help us as we try and navigate life in the absence of our loved ones.

In my grief journey, I felt that sometimes I didn't know what I was feeling and didn't have the words to articulate what was emerging. I hope the book in all those moments reminds you that you are not alone and allows you to be patient with the feelings evoked in you. As you work through your personal journey of navigating grief, I hope this book is a companion and allows your pain to be seen and heard.

May the book allow you to hold grief and hope together.

Acknowledgements

At the age of about nine or ten I knew I wanted to be a psychotherapist. This was also around the time when my dad's health had begun to deteriorate. Now when I think back, my first two jobs in 2004 focused on helping clients deal with loss. Over the last twenty years of work, grief has continued to be a key theme and working on this book was an exercise in putting down all those learnings. This process of writing has been healing and helped me address my own leftover feelings around grief.

It was in 2021 when Diya Kar, an editor I used to work with, suggested this book idea. I'm grateful to Diya for suggesting the idea and believing in me. In the first few months, I worked closely with Sonal Nerurkar, who was the editor on my first book, *Anxiety*. She helped with figuring out how we could structure the book, shared her personal insights and helped with the initial research. Thank you, Sonal, for being a good friend and helping me begin writing this book.

Writing a book requires an entire ecosystem and a village who stands by you. With A Suitable Agency, I found a supporter in Hemali Sodhi right from our first virtual meeting. Her prompt responses, ability to offer nuanced insights and steadfast belief in my work felt reassuring. Once I signed up with A Suitable Agency, I worked closely with Ranjana Sengupta whose calm demeanour, ability to share specific feedback and patience created a beautiful space.

It was a delight to know that the book would be published by Penguin Random House India. Working with Karthik Venkatesh, my editor at Penguin Random House has been a joy. His calmness has been infectious and his capacity to work in a structured manner allowed the work to happen seamlessly. Thank you for the openness to ideas, availability on calls, addressing my doubts and most importantly believing in the book in ways I couldn't myself at an earlier stage. Working with the copy-editing team headed by Saba Nehal, was a joy thanks to her clear communication around timelines, attention to little details. Shweta Kapur and Saba brought curiosity and sensitivity to the process which was so valuable. Sparsh Raj who helped us with design and book cover presented beautiful options and showed an attitude of openness as we worked towards finding a cover design that spoke of both loss and hope.

At a personal level, I have had the immense support of teachers and friends who have all contributed to this journey. Nivedita Chalill, thank you for teaching me what it means to hold space for myself, and offering wisdom in moments when I needed it most. I owe my gratitude to Dr Bharat Shah, Dr Dayal Mirchandani and Dr Anita Sukhwani for being accessible and their attentive presence. Kaushik Gopal, thank you for listening and helping me find a better version of myself over the years. Dr Neeta Jain has been and continues to be a beacon of light as we dealt with grief, and a slew of health emergencies. My aunt Dr Sapna over the years has always a voice of reason and checking in with us.

My friends Parmesh, Aparna, Sunita, Sharon, Arun, Meenal, Ruchita, Anjali, Padmini, Vrinda—thank you for being there in moments when I needed you and offering unconditional support. I feel lucky to have my mum, brother Anupam, sister-in-law Tanvi and Uncle Raman in my life.

My father-in-law passed away while I was still writing this book. Both in his life and death, he taught me how to live. We miss you, your stories, and hope that you are not suffering anymore. Thanks to my mother-in-law for continuing to believe in all the work I do. As I wrote the book, the presence of Laxmi and Geeta allowed for the home to run smoothly and their ability to offer support as we dealt with grief and physical presence has been a gift.

This book wouldn't have been possible without the two people who are the pillars in my life: my husband Gagan and daughter Aneira. I believe writing a book is difficult for the author, but also for the family who is a witness to all of it. Thank you for being patient, tender and loving in all those moments and continuing to do so. The title of the book, creative inputs and idea for the book cover I owe to Gagan. To have a partner who is invested and gently offers suggestions makes the process of writing a little easier. Aneira kept checking about how the writing was progressing and consistently saying the nicest, warmest things that offered me cheer in moments when I was struggling. Thank you, Aneira, for all the love and always being my biggest cheerleader!

To all my clients who trusted me with their personal stories and allowed for some of those experiences to be shared in the book, my thanks. To everyone whom I have had the pleasure of working with, it has been deeply satisfying and a reminder about people's inherent goodness and resilience.

The journey of writing the book has taught me how all our lives are interdependent and a venture as big as a book requires us to trust others, be vulnerable and learn when to lean in. I feel fortunate that so many of you chose to be present and we could work together. What a delightful journey it has been!

Appendix 1

Bereavement Leave/Compassionate Leave

Bereavement leave is the time off/leave given to employees when a loved one dies. The purpose of the bereavement leave is for employees to have time away from their work responsibilities, so that they can attend to the logistical tasks of arranging a funeral or prayer meeting. Most importantly, it is so they can address their own loss and be with their loved ones as they begin to deal with their grief.

When I did some research, I discovered that bereavement leave in India across industries spans anywhere from three to five working days. With companies that offer three to five working days, I was told that employees can combine it with their other sorts of leave to take an extra week or two. However, as I spoke to people across companies, I realized that while employees take time off in case of a loss, there is no official policy around bereavement, with the exception of a few global companies that offer anywhere between two to three weeks of bereavement leave.

The absence of clear policies makes the process of grieving much harder for individuals. Murad, who is forty-two, told me, 'My sister passed away in the summer of 2022. I took the five days off that my company offered, but it was not enough as we had to go to her hometown. So, I extended it by the week. I used my personal leave for that. When I was returning, I came down with high fever and started worrying about not having enough leave days. I felt that I can't even afford to fall sick and just this thought broke me. I had a panic attack and I felt like no one understands how grieving continues, and five days are never enough. While my manager was understanding, he said his hands were tied and since I had exhausted my leave, the HR would count any additional days as unpaid leave.'

Therapy sessions are filled with instances like this, and many more. The problem is when there aren't any clear policies, people don't know what to do. They worry that they will be judged for taking time off and also worry about their salary being cut.

Making a case for compassionate and bereavement leave

What company policies do is normalize certain behaviours and hence, allow for greater support and understanding. At the same time, if a company chooses to give three to five days leave, the understanding is that the employee should come back in that much time, which can be very problematic. Primarily, because processing grief takes much longer and the first few days of loss as we discussed in Chapter 2 come with intense and frequent pain, sorrow and fogginess. The task of playing multiple roles such as lead a team and then attend to funeral logistics and also support other family members can be not just difficult for the grieving individual but also unfair.

That's why in the years to come, we need to acknowledge the urgency to figure out a more humane policy when it comes to bereavement. In a world where we are talking about building emotionally safe spaces and psychological safety, our policies around bereavement leave and the grief literacy training that we offer can go a long way in our employees feeling safe and understood.

Here are a few steps that organizations need to take in the context of bereavement leave, which will offer greater psychological safety to employees:

1. **Clear policies and laws:** Build a clear policy that specifies the number of days that an employee can take off in the aftermath of the loss of a loved one, whether it's a family member, friend, loved one or pet. This should specify whether it's paid leave or unpaid leave. In the absence of clear laws or protocol, it is difficult to navigate these conversations. An act of building a clear bereavement policy is a huge sign that you care for your employees. It shows that, as an organization, you are invested in the employees' well-being, not just their work productivity.
2. **Training in grief literacy:** Training managers, HR and employees at large around grief literacy is crucial. Building programmes for managers, senior management and employees that allow for a culture of compassion and sensitivity and teach employees how to communicate with the bereaved in a manner that's empathetic and supportive helps. A focus on what not to say, how to offer support that's helpful, genuine and ask the right questions is key to building a safe space for employees, who are returning to work after bereavement. Reducing grief stigma at an organizational level is very crucial.
3. **Reducing paperwork and documentation around compassionate leave:** Working out policies and protocols that simplify the process of applying for leave and administrative paperwork can make employees feel supported and understood.

   Building Employee Assistance Programme (EAP) support and extending counselling services to the family in the aftermath of a loss is a step that can help. It normalizes the idea of seeking support.

Offering flexibility, support from managers and an option to take time off as the grieving individual works through the administrative tasks of sorting out paperwork, bank documentation and other chores, which very often have to be done on working days, is another idea that would be appreciated by employees.

4. **Making room for all kinds of loss is essential:** Neelima mentioned how, when she lost her animal companion, she couldn't ask for leave as she didn't know how to. She mentioned how there was no policy around it. When there is disenfranchised grief, people may find it hard to ask or take leave. So, making room for all kinds of loss is crucial, in the context of a miscarriage, people with pets, for those in partnered relationships but not married and in set-ups where there is loss of a colleague or a close friend.

   We need to remember that we spend more than 80 cent of our time at our workplaces. Given that there is a culture of silence and stigma attached to grief, the bereaved individuals have no choice but to stifle their grief and, in turn, not acknowledge what they are going through. **If we want the employees to bring their whole self to work, we need to make room for their grief.**

Appendix 2

The Cost of Death

Chirag, a thirty-three-year-old client who I have been working with for a few years, after his dad's funeral told me, 'Grief is complicated. On the one hand there is sadness, disorientation and an inability to figure out what's happening. On the other hand, there are a thousand things to attend to: logistics around which pandit to call, whether to opt for cremation the old-school way or electric method or whether to use services that exist for last rites or go ahead with what relatives suggest. Amidst all of this I felt overwhelmed and not understood. Mum had a preference, saying that it should be done the old-school way, which I didn't want. I can't begin to tell you how each relative was issuing instructions, about what should be given to the pandit and how food shouldn't be cooked at home till the cremation. All this was getting me irritated, but I put my head down and did it all. I remember feeling torn and bitter by what all comes with grief. Now, with the thirteenth day ceremony done, I can breathe easy. I know it sounds stupid and a cheap thing to say, but grief is expensive, and no one ever tells you that. I haven't worked in fifteen days and yet, whether it's the caterers for the prayer meet, the newspaper obituary or so many other things, I have spent so much money. My business is collapsing, I have my house EMI to pay for and my children's education. I feel that so much expenditure was unnecessary. My father deserved dignity in the way the last rites were done; some of the rituals and caterer business could have been avoided.'

Grief is expensive and no one tells us that.

Costs that come with grief, which we fail to acknowledge

Beena, who is seventy-two, mentioned to me, 'My husband never nominated me for his accounts and then, didn't write a will. I spent hours sitting at the bank trying to close accounts and get my money. My children were all abroad and on so many days, I didn't know if I was exhausted with grief or with the bank work. I was close to giving up this chase, till my son decided to take a sabbatical and come and sort it out. That's when things began to finally move.'

There are costs in the context of administrative tasks, sorting out paperwork and follow-ups that we often don't talk about.

In the report titled, 'Cost of Dying 2024 Report' by www.empathy.com, researchers have shared, 'The average person took fifteen months to complete all the administrative tasks to wrap up their loved one's affairs or eighteen months if they were the executor of the estate.'

In the context of stress, the report states, 'At least 94.5 per cent reported suffering from at least one negative physical or mental symptom after their loss and 84 per cent said these symptoms had a harmful impact on their daily life.'[1]

My experience has been that some grieving individuals I worked with have taken anywhere between a couple of years to a decade to sort out matters around finances and property, particularly if there was no nomination, or when the family had no knowledge about where the money was invested. These administrative tasks require immense monotasking, alertness and taking time out from one's work or caregiving duties. As a result, they leave the grieving individual exhausted and consistently overwhelmed.

When it comes to stress, in my therapy experience, couples and individuals who are grieving in the first few months report various interpersonal struggles, such as breakdown of communication, conflict over how things are to be sorted, bouts of irritability, anger and frustration as they try and make sense of their grief and the logistics that come with it.

These costs, whether visible or not, are a reminder that grief is not just an individual problem to be dealt with—it requires an entire ecosystem of support, laws and regulations at multiple levels for grieving individuals to feel supported.

Notes

2. What Is Grief?

1 Colin Murray Parkes and Holly G. Prigerson, *Bereavement: Studies of Grief in Adult Life*, illustrated and revised edition (London: Routledge, 2013), p. 6.
2 *The Standard Edition of the Complete Works of Sigmund Freud*, translated from the German under the editorship of James Strachey in collaboration with Anna Freud, volume XIV (1914–1916) (London: Hogarth Press and Institute of Psychoanalysis), p. 243.
3 Victor Yalom, 'Kenneth Doka on Grief Counseling and Psychotherapy', Psychotherapy, https://www.psychotherapy.net/interview/grief-counseling-doka.

3. The Vocabulary around Loss

1 'Episode 184, How Grieving Changes the Brain', *Speaking of Psychology*, produced by the American Psychological Association, https://www.apa.org/news/podcasts/speaking-of-psychology/grieving-changes-brain. Mary Frances O'Connor makes this distinction.
2 Sidney Zisook and Katherine Shear, 'Grief and Bereavement: What Psychiatrists Need To Know', *World Psychiatry: Official Journal of the World Psychiatric Association* 8 (2) (2009): 67–74, https://pubmed.ncbi.nlm.nih.gov/19516922/.

3 'Bereavement', APA Dictionary of Psychology, https://dictionary.apa.org/bereavement.
4 B.A. Mulemi, 'Mourning and Grieving', in D. Leeming (eds), *Encyclopedia of Psychology and Religion* (Berlin: Springer, 2017).
5 Nicola K.S. Davis, 'Mourning rituals help people cope with grief, say scientists', *Guardian*, 11 September 2022, https://www.theguardian.com/society/2022/sep/11/mourning-rituals-help-people-cope-with-grief-scientists.

7. Models of Grief

1 Dr Elisabeth Kübler-Ross and David Kessler, *On Grief and Grieving: Finding the Meaning of Grief through the Five Stages of Loss* (New York: Simon and Schuster, 2014), p. 10.
2 Ibid., p. 22.
3 David Kessler, *Finding Meaning: The Sixth Stage of Grief* (New York: Simon and Schuster, 2019).
4 *The Standard Edition of the Complete Psychological Works of Sigmund Freud*, translated from German under the general editorship of James Strachey in collaboration with Annua Freud (London: Hogarth Press and Institute of Psychoanalysis), pp. 234–44.
5 Robert Neimeyer et al., 'Grief Therapy and the Reconstruction of Meaning: From Principles to Practice', *Journal of Contemporary Psychotherapy* 40 (2010): 73–83.

8. There Is No Hierarchy

1 Brené Brown, *Atlas of the Heart: Mapping Meaningful Connection and the Language of Human Experience*, (London: Penguin Random House UK, 2021), pp. 130–31.

9. What If My Loved One Dies?

1 Sonali Gupta, 'Anticipatory Grief', *Mumbai Mirror*, 11 February 2019, https://mumbaimirror.indiatimes.com/mumbai/other/anticipatory-grief/articleshow/67935036.cms

11. Vicarious Grief

1 Sonali Gupta, 'Why you should address vicarious grief', *Mint Lounge,* 15 May 2021, https://lifestyle.livemint.com/relationships/it-s-complicated/how-to-address-vicarious-grief-111621050053061.html

2 Robert Kastenbaum, 'Vicarious Grief: An Intergenerational Phenomenon?', *Death Studies* 11(6) (1987): 447–53, https://www.tandfonline.com/doi/abs/10.1080/07481188708252209?journalCode=udst20

3 Sonali Gupta, 'Why you should address vicarious grief', *Mint Lounge,* 15 May 2021, https://lifestyle.livemint.com/relationships/it-s-complicated/how-to-address-vicarious-grief-111621050053061.html

13. Traumatic Grief

1 A.G. De Leon Corona et al., 'The Virulence of Grief in the Pandemic: Bereavement Overload During COVID.' *American Journal of Hospice and Palliative Medicine* 39(10) (2022):1244–49; A.H. Kutscher and R. Kastenbaum 'Death and bereavement in later life'. In: *Death and Bereavement*. Springfield, Illinois: Charles C. Thomas; 1974: 28–54; R.A. Neimeyer and J.M. Holland. 'Encyclopedia of human development.' (2006).

16. The Culture of Silence

1 Katherine May, *Wintering: The Power of Rest and Retreat in Difficult Times* (London: Penguin Random House UK, 2020), p. 9.

18. No One Grieves the Same Way

1 David Kessler, *Finding Meaning: The Sixth Stage of Grief* (New York: Simon and Schuster 2019), p. 29.

20. Grief Activators

1 Eleanor Haley, 'Grief Triggers and Positive Memory: A Continuum', What's Your Grief, https://whatsyourgrief.com/grief-triggers-positive-memories-continuum/.

24. You Are More than Your Grief

1 Nora Mclnerny, 'We Don't "Move On" from Grief. We Move Forward with It.', TED Women 2018, November 2018, https://www.ted.com/talks/nora_mcinerny_we_don_t_move_on_from_grief_we_move_forward_with_it?language=en.

27. All the What-Ifs

1 Dr Elisabeth Kübler-Ross and David Kessler, *On Grief and Grieving: Finding the Meaning of Grief through the Five Stages of Loss* (New York: Simon Schuster, 2014), p. 17.
2 Eleanor Haley, '"How Old Would She Be Now?" and Other Grief Equations', What's Your Grief, https://whatsyourgrief.com/grief-math-and-grief-equations/.
3 'hindsight bias', APA Dictionary of Psychology, https://dictionary.apa.org/hindsight-bias.

29. Mixed Feelings

1 Esther Perel and Mary Alice Walker, 'The Myth of Unconditional Love in Romantic Relationships', https://www.estherperel.com/blog/the-myth-of-unconditional-love-in-romantic-relationships.

30. Closure

1 Pauline Boss, *The Myth of Closure: Ambiguous Loss in a Time of Pandemic and Change* (London: WW Norton & Co, 2021).

31. Dreams

1 Patricia Tevington and Manolo Corichi, 'Many Americans report interacting with dead relatives in dreams or other ways', Pew Research, 23 August 2023, https://www.pewresearch.org/short-reads/2023/08/23/many-americans-report-interacting-with-dead-relatives-in-dreams-or-other-ways/#:~:text=Many%20Americans%20report%20that%20their,dream%20or%20some%20other%20form.

32. What Do We Want to Hear from Friends and Family?

1 Hugh Hollowell, 'Grief Groceries', http://hughlh.com/grief-groceries/.

33. What Doesn't Work and What Not to Say

1 Brené Brown, *Atlas of the Heart: Mapping Meaningful Connection and Language of Human Experience* (London: Penguin Random House UK, 2021), p. 123.

Appendix 2: The Cost of Death

1 Empathy.com is a platform that helps families navigate the emotional and logistical challenges of loss: https://www.empathy.com/costofdying.

Bibliography

Research Papers and Magazine, Journal and Newspaper Articles

'The Myth of Closure and Grief', Grief Plan, https://www.griefplan.com/videos-blog-1/the-myth-of-closure-amp-grief.

Conrad Collaco, 'Why we have grief dreams when a loved one dies and what dreams might mean', CBC News, 20 December 2018, https://www.cbc.ca/news/canada/hamilton/grief-dreams-1.4953715.

David Kessler, 'The high costs of grief literacy', Quartz, 25 October 2021, https://qz.com/2078527/the-high-costs-of-grief-illiteracy.

Eleanor Haley, 'Closure isn't a thing in grief and that's okay', What's Your Grief, 2 February 2021, https://whatsyourgrief.com/closure-isnt-a-thing-in-grief-and-thats-okay/.

Kaina Marie Clare Sera Jose et al., 'Bereaved in Me: Understanding the Vicarious Grief Experiences Among Helping Professionals During the COVID-19 Pandemic', *National Library of Medicine,* 13 January 2023, https://www.ncbi.nlm.nih.gov/pmc/articles/PMC9841206/#:~:text=Vicarious%20grief%20(VG)%20refers%20to,not%20personally%20known%20by%20them.

Katie C. Reilly, 'When birthdays, songs, other things can spark grief long after a loved one's death', *Washington Post,* 2 October 2021, https://www.washingtonpost.com/health/

grief-triggers-activators/2021/10/01/e7d84560-164f-11ec-a5e5-ceecb895922f_story.html#-.

Kenneth J. Doka, 'Disenfranchised grief in historical and cultural perspective', APA PsycNet, https://psycnet.apa.org/record/2008-09330-011.

Mary-Frances O'Connor, 'Grief: A Brief History of Research on How Body, Mind and Brain Adapt', *Psychosomatic Medicine* 81 (8) (2019): 731–38, https://www.ncbi.nlm.nih.gov/pmc/articles/PMC6844541/.

Meg Bernhard, 'What if there is no such thing as closure', 15 December 2021, *New York Times*, https://www.nytimes.com/2021/12/15/magazine/grieving-loss-closure.html.

Pauline Boss, 'Navigating loss without closure', Being, 16 July 2020, https://onbeing.org/programs/pauline-boss-navigating-loss-without-closure/.

Rita DeMontis, 'The grief phenomena of strange dreaming', *Toronto Sun,* 14 June 2021, https://torontosun.com/life/relationships/the-strange-phenomena-of-grief-dreaming.

Sonali Gupta, 'Love, loss and longing in times of coronavirus', *Mumbai Mirror,* 30 March 2020, https://mumbaimirror.indiatimes.com/coronavirus/news/love-loss-and-longing-in-times-of-coronavirus/articleshow/74880704.cms.

Sonali Gupta, 'The grief of childlessness for those who want kids', *Hindustan Times,* 18 April 2023, www.hindustantimes.com/cities/mumbai-news/the-hidden-grief-of-infertility-understanding-disenfranchised-grief-and-the-need-for-support-amidst-a-society-s-implicit-expectations-infertility--disenfranchisedgrief-support-101681759992286.html.

Victoria A. Brownworth, 'Grief: A Mental Health Crisis for LGBTQ People', *Philadelphia Gay News,* 25 May 2023, https://epgn.com/2023/05/25/grief-a-mental-health-crisis-for-lgbtq-people/.

Victoria A. Brownworth, 'LGBTQ self-care during COVID-19', *Philadelphia Gay News,* 15 April 2020, https://epgn.com/2020/04/15/lgbtq-self-care-during-covid-19/.

Books

Atul Gawande, *Being Mortal: Medicine and What Matters in the End* (New York: Metropolitan Books, Henry Holt and Company, 2014).

Elisabeth Kübler-Ross MD and David Kessler, *Life Lessons: Two Experts on Death and Dying Teach Us About the Mysteries of Life and Living* (New York: Scribner, 2014).

Oliver Jeffers, *Heart and The Bottle* (New York: Philomel Books, 2010).

Reports and Audio-Visual References

'Finding Meaning in Grief: Robert Niemeyer in conversation with Lesel Dawson', YouTube, 27 September 2022, https://youtu.be/6r28S6iZ3Yc?si=VcRnAx4sYXC6FBgb.

'The Cost of Dying', report by Empathy, 2024, https://www.empathy.com/costofdying.

Pauline Boss, 'Navigating Loss without Closure', On Being with Krista Tipett, podcast, original airdate 23 June 2016, https://onbeing.org/programs/pauline-boss-navigating-loss-without-closure/.

Scan QR code to access the
Penguin Random House India website